Getting Between the Balance Sheets

Getting Between the Balance Sheets

The Four Things Every Entrepreneur Should Know About Finance

David Frodsham
Entrepreneur, CEO, Adviser and Board member

Heinrich Liechtenstein
Professor of Finance, IESE, Spain

First published 2011 by
PALGRAVE MACMILLAN

Palgrave Macmillan in the UK is an imprint of Macmillan Publishers Limited, registered in England, company number 785998, of Houndmills, Basingstoke, Hampshire RG21 6XS.

Palgrave Macmillan in the US is a division of St Martin's Press LLC, 175 Fifth Avenue, New York, NY 10010.

Palgrave Macmillan is the global academic imprint of the above companies and has companies and representatives throughout the world.

Palgrave® and Macmillan® are registered trademarks in the United States, the United Kingdom, Europe and other countries.

ISBN: 978–0–230–25286–8 hardback

This book is printed on paper suitable for recycling and made from fully managed and sustained forest sources. Logging, pulping and manufacturing processes are expected to conform to the environmental regulations of the country of origin.

A catalogue record for this book is available from the British Library.

A catalog record for this book is available from the Library of Congress.

10 9 8 7 6 5 4 3 2 1
20 19 18 17 16 15 14 13 12 11

Printed and bound in Great Britain by
CPI Antony Rowe, Chippenham and Eastbourne

Contents

Preface

If business were a sport, finance could be one of your top goal-scorers.

An entrepreneur needs to be able to run his or her company with numbers in a way that cannot be delegated to the CFO or company accountant. External investors, partners and potential purchasers of a venture want to talk about finance and they only really want to speak to the entrepreneur.

We wrote this book because we have both been entrepreneurs and would have loved a book on entrepreneurial finance. Finance, which is about using financial information to make better business decisions, is not to be confused with accounting, the process of keeping track of the financial performance of a company.

If finance can be thought of as a goal-scorer, accounting would be the score-keeper.

Just four items determine whether an entrepreneur's venture will succeed financially, meaning all the stakeholders make money: the founders, their investors and the staff through stock options. These four items are all connected with the balance sheet.

But few entrepreneurs spend as much time on them as they do on building products and a customer base. They might not even be aware of what they are. Being an entrepreneur is a lonely, adrenalin-filled fight against seemingly unrelenting adversity. A little financial knowledge, planning and action at the right time can make all the difference.

At its simplest, a balance sheet consists of items that need funding ("assets") and items that provide the funding ("liabilities and equity"). There may be surplus cash or a line of credit, but that is it. That makes balance sheets easy to understand and to analyse. This leads us to the four items that determine a venture's financial success. They are:

- How is the cash that is needed to run the company estimated, managed and reduced? Everyone has heard of "working capital" but rather like the word "marketing" it means different things to different people. Very few have a strategic objective to reduce the cash tied up in the company and fewer make it a key element in product management and other business decision-making. We present a complete and easy to use approach, together with a set of tools in order to tie up less cash in the company's operations.
- How is the cake to be sliced between entrepreneur and investor? The "cake" is the proceeds from the sale of the business rather than the relative percentage shareholdings. There are many examples of successful companies where the entrepreneur realizes too late that owning say 40 per cent of the

company that is being sold for €20 million does not mean a cheque for €8 million; in fact it could mean getting nothing at all. Thanks to a comprehensive survey of European VCs, we show how to protect value for the founders when negotiating a VC term sheet. VCs and entrepreneurs alike agree that the size of the cake should be more important than the size of the slice, but percentage ownership has normally little to do with how the economic value of the company is divided up.

- How should staff be rewarded, in order to attract top talent at perhaps less than market rates? Share options have had a bad press recently, but the main reason is that they all too rarely result in the option holders making money. Using an equity exit model, we show how to create a good share option plan and how to sell it to investors. Without this, start-ups will either pay money they can't afford for the right talent or not hire the right people.

- How to get the best outcome at a liquidity event, such as selling the company? There is one shot to get the valuation right and the company sold to the right bidder. But more often than not the investors and management will fight about whether to sell the company now or to wait, to whom and for how much, because each has different objectives. An exit is in fact not a door to outside, but a door to a different place. Instead of an "exit", we prefer to call it a liquidity event: a time when some or all of the shareholders get to convert some or all of their ownership into cash.

Blockbuster start-ups that are sold for gazillions may not need to worry about these points too much, because the multiples they are sold for disguise any financial structural problems. But the vast majority of ventures provide a more modest return and mastering these four items can make the difference between personal financial success and failure.

To illustrate these four points and how they can be addressed, we follow the story of a mythical first-time entrepreneur, Grace Inge. She has a blockbuster product and a high media profile. Fuelled by personal ambition and the world's attention, she lurches from one crisis to another, some of which are solvable and some not. The book is divided into episodes, each telling part of her story, and chapters, that explain the financial issues behind the episode.

Grace is not a real person; she is an amalgam of a number of real entrepreneurs that we have met. Her company, MissInge Fashions, is fictitious, but the company's figures are based on real companies. The incidents are disguised but are based on real events, mostly from technology companies rather than from the fashion industry, of course. We chose the fashion industry rather than something more high-tech to illustrate that the issues of wealth creation and entrepreneurship remain the same, whatever the product and industry.

Otherwise all the characters, names and companies are fictitious and are not based on any real person, company or situation.

Acknowledgements

Our thanks go in particular to Christiane Reuter, Daniel Reilly, Lauren Thomas and Sergiy Dmytriyev who helped with the survey of Venture Capital firms in Europe, and to Karsten Lieser for helping with the many graphs and tables.

We acknowledge Professor Eduardo Martinez Abascal's insight into sustainable growth rates, and others in the Finance Department of IESE for their work on NFO.

The CEO Collaborative Forum has been a vital source of entrepreneur war stories and we are grateful for their support.

We extend our thanks to the many people who helped check the book for accuracy, consistency and flow.

David Frodsham
and
Heinrich Liechtenstein

Episode 1
And the Winner is…
MissInge Fashions!

10 September 2009

This is not going to go down as the most exciting dinner in Grace's life. The man on her right is a Nordic designer of incomprehensibly complicated but undoubtedly worthy wireless electronic gadgets. The man on her left is trying to create a social network of some sort. He seems to be too young to have even left school and doesn't seem interested in fashion. The three don't have much in common and everyone else at the table is too far away to talk to.

Grace sighs, pulls out her iPhone and starts looking at her email. There's such a lot going on that she needs every moment in the day to keep on top of the whirlwind growth the company is enjoying. Being sent by marketing to an awards dinner is just another opportunity.

She founded the eponymous MissInge Fashions two years ago, but this year the company is really being transformed. By the end of next year it will no longer be a cottage industry but a global, high-profile brand. It feels good.

There is no doubt in her mind about the reason for the success: the Carrera jacket. Made from next-generation microfibre and designed by MissInge's extraordinarily talented team in Biella, Italy, it has become the year's must-have fashion item. Celebrities are photographed coming out of the coolest nightclubs wearing them, eBay has a special section selling them, and there are regularly queues outside fashion stores when new variants are released. Lots of fashion houses are trying to copy the Carrera jacket, but none has managed to achieve the cachet and high prices of the original.

A couple of months ago the Carrera jacket won Product of the Year, and earlier in the year she had been awarded VC Backed Entrepreneur of the Year. She seemed to be somewhere on the web, television or in print every week. Publicity is great for business.

Yes, it feels really good.

There's an upbeat sales report from Joe. He is on target to double sales compared with last year, but more importantly for sales to rise fourfold next year. That big step is pretty much assured, now that reseller agreements are in place with the country's key retail chains. Sales will also shortly start in Russia and Japan – both fashion-conscious markets. The launch is in the final stages of planning and the PR machine is starting to promote Grace as a personality. Joe just wants reassuring the company can supply everything his sales team is selling.

Joe is quite a catch as head of sales. Grace had poached him from one of the big fashion houses, where he was in one of the top business development roles. Attracted by a fat share option package, Joe knows everyone in the fashion industry and is one of the main reasons sales are growing so quickly. He can be a little difficult and a bit coin-operated for her liking, but otherwise he's a key member of her senior management team.

Joe's concerns about production shouldn't be an issue, she thought. With the €4 million MissInge had raised from the investors earlier in the year, at a great valuation, production had been increased and there was a new warehouse, with all the latest logistics equipment, coming on stream. She was about to draw down the final €2 million; she just needed a piece of paper from the bank, which shouldn't be a problem.

Grace had always wanted her company to have its own building, with a brass plaque on the front, and now she had it. It made the company feel more important, more permanent and solid. Mary, the logistics guru, had been in her office earlier in the day, very confident about meeting demand. Production quality coming from the factory in China was good and the new production line was on stream after some teething problems. The supply chain is long, and good sales forecasting vital as MissInge commits months ahead to production.

Grace looks up as the waiter comes round, refuses the dessert but accepts a glass of wine instead and continues to read her email.

The marketing department has sent through a draft of her latest blog entry *MissInge in Action* and a collection of the latest extensive press clippings. There seem to be no limit to the number of people who want to meet her, and write about her and MissInge. She decides to read it later.

There's a note from Dan, her "angel" shareholder, who backed the company in the early days with a very generous €300,000 investment. She could not have built the company without him. He congratulates her on an article on MissInge he has just read.

She sits back, looking pleased. Thank goodness the company is doing so well after two years of really hard work. She's at the top of her game, the pinnacle of everything she had worked so hard for. She smiles at the thought of how proud her parents are of her.

There's an email from accounts.

From: (Accounts Receivable >)

Bank manager called

10 September 2009 17:07

Hi Grace

Hans at the bank has called several times and wants you to call back, even if it's out of hours and on his mobile. It's urgent apparently. He's also sent you a text.
Have fun tonight – bring home some silverware!

Sally
Accounts Receivable
MissInge Fashions

Grace looks at her unread text messages.

> Grace, please call ASAP, I have an update from loan committee. Call any time. Hans.

Grace looks around, but nothing much is happening yet. It's a bit late to call the bank manager, but he did say call at any time. She stands up from the table and moves to a discreet spot at the side, just outside the room.

She wonders what it can possibly be. It can't be the financial performance; after all, revenue is higher and costs lower than plan. All Hans has to do is sign the form that was agreed as part of the last round of funding. The bank is to provide a €500,000 working capital credit line at the same time as the final €2 million of equity is released from the investors. It's all agreed; there can't be an issue. And he needs to do it now; otherwise the company is going to hit a wall cash-wise in a matter of days.

"Hans Schmidt," says Hans as he answers his mobile.

"Hans, this is Grace," she whispers back. "Sorry to phone so late, but it sounded urgent."

"Thank you for phoning back, Grace. I've been trying to reach you for some time, but I can never get through; you're so busy. We're not going to extend the credit line, even if that means shutting MissInge down. I'm so sorry."

"But, Hans, I don't understand. Why ... ?"

"Have you seen your balance sheet?"

"Balance sheet? What do you mean?" asks Grace, incredulously. "You can't do this, Hans, this will kill the company."

"We need to meet. Can we talk tomorrow? I'm sorry to ruin your evening." Hans clearly does not want to go into any detail late at night over the phone.

"Can you email me the details first?" asks Grace, deeply shocked.

"I'll email you tomorrow morning and let's meet soon after that."

"OK, bye for now."

As Grace hangs up, there's a tap on her shoulder. It's her dinner partner, the electronics expert.

"They're calling you, Grace. You've won an award."

"An award?"

"Yes. *The Small Company Most Likely to Succeed.*"

Chapter 1
Cash is King

Revenue is vanity, profit is sanity but cash is reality.

Business maxim

One Dilbert strip, ever able to lampoon corporate life, runs like this: "I've been saying for years that employees are our most valuable asset. It turns out I was wrong, money is our most valuable asset." Without forgetting the importance of staff, strategy, timing and many other things that are key to a start-up's success, the only way perhaps to improve Dilbert's cartoon would be to replace the word "money" with the word "cash".

Companies don't fail because of losses; they fail because they run out of cash. Think of cash as the air of business: without it, a company cannot live long. With cash, a company can have products available for sale when customers want to buy them; it can invest in new products and services, and pay its staff and suppliers on time. It might be able to provide a cash income to its shareholders in the form of a dividend.

Without enough cash a company may stumble along for some time, but eventually it will lose out to better-funded competitors.

Unprofitable companies will sooner or later run out of cash because they lose money. But profitable companies can run out of cash too, especially if they are fast-growing and investing in the future faster than they are generating profits from past business. Profits become cash but that can take a very long time, so in the short term, profits and cash are not the same.

The easiest way to look at profits is through the Profit and Loss (P&L) account but the Balance Sheet is the best place to see how cash is moving and being managed.

Good cash flow can disguise a bad business. Take a hypothetical example of an on-demand Internet retailer that buys its stock from suppliers on 60 days' terms but gets instant payment from its customers. Competitive pressure means the company sells the products at such low prices that the gross

5

profit is smaller than the operating costs. For the first 60 days of trading, there is plenty of cash coming in from customers and little going out because suppliers are not due to be paid yet. Over time, once cumulated losses are larger than the value of the 60 days of supplier credit, the cash received from today's customers would not be enough to pay the supplier and the e-tailer would run out of cash and go bust. But it would take a while.

Most businesses need cash to grow, irrespective of how profitable they are. Today's cash comes from yesterday's business, but is spent preparing the company for tomorrow's business. If the company is growing quickly, this can consume more cash than the amount generated by profits. Some companies, like insurance companies or supermarkets, generate more cash than profits as they grow, mainly because their customers pay them before they have to pay their suppliers. Insurance companies might wait years before paying out claims, during which time they are sitting on their customers' premiums.

Companies that generate cash faster than profits are rare exceptions to the basic rule that cash arrives after profits are made and this causes big problems for early-stage growth companies.

Cash is the most important financial metric for entrepreneurs and the balance sheet is the best place to understand what the cash dynamics of any business are. It is for example possible to calculate the sustainable growth rate of a business – making sure the cash generated from profits equals the cash consumed in new growth – by looking at its balance sheet.

Cash is the key financial metric for entrepreneurs, or rather it should be. Cash should be at the heart of product planning, product management and sales, as well as the company's business plan.

To understand why, we need to return to Grace's predicament.

Episode 2

MissInge's Balance Sheet

Happiness: a good bank account, a good cook and a good digestion.

Jean-Jacques Rousseau

From: Hans Schmidt
Sent: 11 September 2009 09:20
To: Grace Inge
Subject: Balance sheet

Good morning, Grace,

I am sorry about spoiling your moment of triumph last night – it must have confirmed your worst nightmares about bankers. I just had to let you know the decision of the loan committee.

Our concern is the alarming rise in a number of assets, especially inventory. This is of course combined with a drop in cash reserves which, as you recently shared with me your ambitious growth targets, rang an alarm bell. So I looked into your balance sheet further.

Frankly, Grace, I am so worried that I have to stop you, right now. I am convinced that you have to change radically and to do so immediately or you (and of course the bank) are going to have a real crisis on your hands.

I have managed to get a short stay of execution in that my regional manager has agreed to review the decision in 30 days' time if we can make real progress in resolving the problems and we sort out a plan of action. (It perhaps helped that we did that case study on you in the last issue of the bank's internal newsletter and we do like dealing with people in the public eye. But it has to make financial sense for us all.)

Time is not on our side, so take a look at the attached analysis (I've highlighted the key bits) and let's have a meeting as soon as you have a plan for how to address the problem.

Best regards,

Hans Schmidt, Strategic Corporate Accounts Director
The Bank for Entrepreneurs

** "Bank of the Year": Winner 2008, Finalist 2009 **

Missinge Fashions

P&L in €000			2007	2008	2009	2010	2011	2012	2013
			Recent Years			Forecast			
Sales		(1)	180	1,350	2,592	10,653	16,022	19,373	23,248
Raw material Microfibre			−65	−473	−855	−3,409	−4,807	−5,812	−6,974
Raw material others			−41	−305	−570	−2,301	−3,365	−4,068	−4,882
Manufacturing			−27	−203	−311	−1,087	−1,634	−1,976	−2,371
shipping (percentage of sales)	2.8%		−5	−38	−73	−298	−449	−542	−651
Gross margin			42	332	783	3,558	5,768	6,974	8,369
Personnel costs		(2)	−280	−560	−2,170	−2,520	−3,080	−3,430	−4,130
Operating costs as % of Headcount	40%	(3)	−112	−224	−868	−1,008	−1,232	−1,372	−1,652
EBITDA			−350	−452	−2,255	30	1,456	2,172	2,587
Depreciation	25%	(4)	0	−5	−34	−518	−963	−957	−865
EBIT			−350	−457	−2,289	−488	493	1,215	1,723
Financial expenses net	13%	(5)	0	0	0	0	−460	−664	−677
EBT			−350	−457	−2,289	−488	33	551	1,045
GM			23%	25%	30%	33%	36%	36%	36%

Balance (€000)			2007	2008	2009	2010	2011	2012	2013
			Recent Years			Forecast			
Cash		(6)	421	1,927	1,405	0	0	0	0
Inventories			40	297	532	2,095	3,017	3,648	4,377
Raw Material		(7)	8	56	102	408	581	702	843
Work in Progress	12	(8)	4	29	53	208	300	362	435
Finished Goods			29	212	377	1,478	2,136	2,583	3,100
Receivables			30	225	432	1,776	2,670	3,229	3,875
Current Assets			491	2,450	2,368	3,870	5,687	6,877	8,252
Fixed Assets			20	135	2,071	3,853	3,830	3,459	3,272
TOTAL ASSETS			511	2,585	4,440	7,724	9,517	10,335	11,524
Credit			0	0	0	3,537	5,105	5,210	5,165
Trade payables		(9)	3	25	48	192	280	339	407
Accruals	35%	(10)	8	16	63	74	90	100	120
Current liabilities			12	42	111	3,802	5,475	5,649	5,693
Government soft loan	7.5%	(11)	500	1,000	1,075	1,156	1,242	1,335	1,436
Share capital (Founders + Angel)			350	350	350	350	350	350	350
Share capital investors			0	2,000	6,000	6,000	6,000	6,000	6,000
Equity			0	1,543	3,254	2,766	2,799	3,350	4,396
TOTAL LIABILITIES AND EQUITY			511	2,585	4,440	7,724	9,517	10,335	11,524

Operational Finance	Recent Years			Forecast			
	2007	2008	2009	2010	2011	2012	2013
NFO	59	481	853	3,605	5,317	6,437	7,725
WC	480	2,408	2,258	68	212	1,227	2,559
Cash surplus (+), Credit (−)	421	1,927	1,405	−3,537	−5,105	−5,210	−5,165

Chapter 2
Balance Sheet Beauty

What I dream of is an art of balance.

Henri Matisse

The balance sheet's elegance comes from the simple idea that what you're worth (your "equity") is what you own ("assets") minus what you owe ("liabilities"). Or, in balance sheet terms, assets equal your liabilities plus equity. Not just simple, but powerful, as we will see.

Balance sheets can look quite different depending on the country of the company, which accounting standard is used and the way a company chooses to present the data. The great thing is that the underlying idea and information are all the same, just laid out differently. So with a little effort, you can look at any balance sheet from anywhere and understand it.

Here's the style of balance sheet we prefer and will use (Appendix 3 contains an explanation of balance sheet terms):

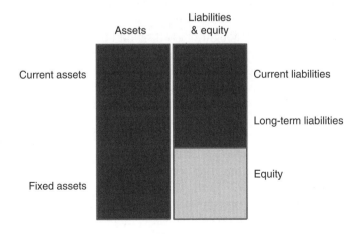

The balance sheet – with assets on the left and liabilities on the right side – is often used to refer to how strong a company is. A company has "a strong balance sheet". It's easy, isn't it? Assets are "good", while liabilities are "bad", as the names imply. All you need is lots of assets and few liabilities and the company will be better.

In fact, rather the reverse is true. Assets need to be funded: an increase in assets in the above balance sheet while keeping everything else the same can only be achieved by a reduction in cash. Conversely, liabilities reduce the amount of funding needed or increase the cash level of the company. Or, put more simply, assets need funding and liabilities provide funding.

If someone owes you money for work you have done or products you have provided – creating a "receivable", which is an asset – your company is out of pocket: it has spent money but not yet received any back. If, on the other hand, you haven't paid a supplier yet – creating a "payable", which is a liability – it means you have been given their products free for a while, which helps to fund your business.

Assets can be funded either by an increase in liabilities, or by shareholders investing more equity. Out of those two only an increase in liabilities sounds even slightly attractive; even then the company needs to be able to afford the liability comfortably.

The recent global financial crisis has shown that having too many liabilities can bring great companies to earth and we are not advocating an extreme increase in liabilities. With apologies for the pun, it's a question of balance.

Liabilities can be a very good thing indeed, provided of course that the company is well equipped to withstand a crisis and the risk of bankruptcy is small. To discourage their customers from abusing the privilege of credit, suppliers often give a discount for early payment of invoices, prompting a decision between paying less money earlier, or more money later. Or in our terms, a choice between more cash or more profit.

Even cash should not be thought of as all "good", because it too needs to be funded by an increase in liabilities or equity. If surplus cash (beyond a prudent buffer) is just going to sit in the company's bank earning a small amount of interest, why is this cash in the company and not with the shareholders? Investors would rather have surplus cash in their own accounts, rather than in the company's.

Again, because balance sheets have to balance, a company with surplus cash has too much equity. So profits are spread across more shares, reducing profit per share. For this reason companies sometimes use surplus cash to buy back their own shares.

With less cash and fewer assets, provided it does not excessively weaken the balance sheet, a company would be financially more successful and the shareholders would be wealthier.

Let's go back to the point when MissInge was founded and build the balance sheet back up to where it is today.

Grace founds her company, MissInge Fashions, with an initial share capital of €50,000. She opens a bank account and deposits the €50,000 in cash for her shares. The balance sheet then just has €50,000 cash on the left and €50,000 equity on the right:

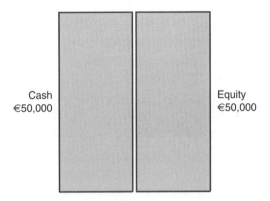

She then uses some of the cash to buy a piece of equipment (a fixed asset) for €10,000:

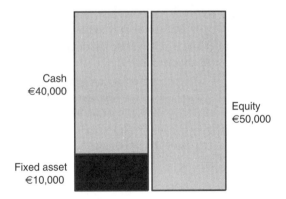

Then she starts to trade.

To get her company going, she buys products from other companies and sells them at a 50 per cent mark-up. Her supplier is happy to be paid in 30 days.

The first step is to buy €10,000 of inventory, which creates two new balance sheet items, one on each side. Inventory is the value of the product that has been bought and payables is the liability to pay the supplier.

Here's the balance sheet:

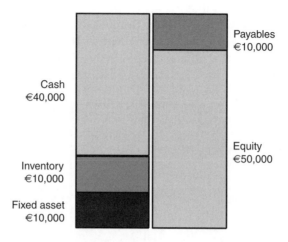

Nothing so far has changed the equity position, nor, other than buying the fixed asset, has the cash level changed. The balance sheet has become bigger, which has no significance as to how well the company is doing, other than to show that there are more items that provide funding (the payables) and an identical item that needs funding (the inventory).

Next, Grace sells the inventory at a profit to a customer who will pay her later. The Inventory item disappears and is replaced with a larger €15,000 Receivables item (remember she is selling the product at a 50 per cent mark-up, or 150 per cent of the cost of the inventory):

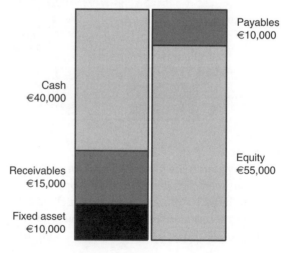

The equity has also increased – this is where profits are accumulated. This is shown here as a single item, although it is normal to differentiate between Share Capital, the amount the investors have invested, and Retained Earnings, being the accumulated profits of the company, less any dividends.

In due course the supplier is paid and the customer pays. The balance sheet now goes back to how it was, just with a little more cash on the left and a little more equity on the right, being the amount of profit that has been made.

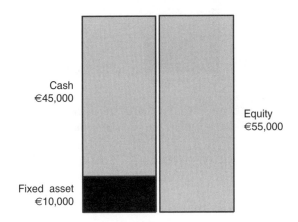

But that does not help Grace to build a business that is selling on an ongoing basis. She needs to have products available for sale all the time, so decides that having about a month and a half of sales demand in stock will enable her to meet the lumpy orders she expects. That might sound a lot, but illustratively if she wants to start by selling 100 jackets a month it wouldn't be unreasonable to have 150 in stock, bearing in mind different sizes and perhaps colours. (We're assuming here they all cost the same.)

Let's consider the cash implications for monthly sales of €15,000, with COGS (the Cost of Goods Sold) of €10,000 and therefore a margin of €5,000:

- She pays the supplier for 30 days' worth of sales, so payables will be €10,000.
- There are 45 days of inventory, valued therefore at €15,000.
- Receivables will be €15,000, being the equivalent of one month's sales.

This is the balance sheet we developed above, with the new elements added:

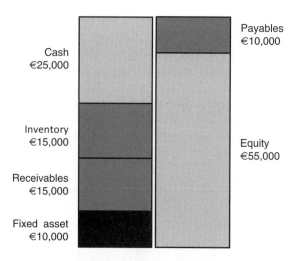

The funding needed for operations is simply the items on the left of the balance sheet that need funding less the items on the right that provide funding, so:

€15,000 inventory + €15,000 receivables − €10,000 payables
= €20,000 funding needed for operations.

MissInge's cash balance now stands at €25,000, being the €45,000 balance from her original transaction less the €20,000 funding needed for the operations.

Her monthly sales are €15,000; €180,000 annually. Her €20,000 funding requirement is equivalent to 11 per cent of annual sales.

Another way of looking at this is that every time sales increase by €100, an additional funding of €11 is needed.

Funds needed for each sale we will refer to as the "Necessary Funds for Operations", or NFO.[1] NFO is defined as necessary cash + Inventory + Receivables − Payables and other items that depend on sales. It answers the question of how much funding is needed every time a company sells something. For most companies, NFO is a large part of a company's balance sheet.

So our balance sheet can be simplified into four categories:

- Cash surplus (remember necessary cash is included in the NFO)
- NFO

[1] What we refer to here as NFO, some people might call working capital (WC), net working capital (NWC), working capital requirement (WCR) or even operating working capital (OWC). However, there are many different concepts behind each of those expressions, so for clarity we have chosen NFO, an approach developed in IESE.

- Fixed assets
- Equity.

Here is MissInge's simplified balance sheet:

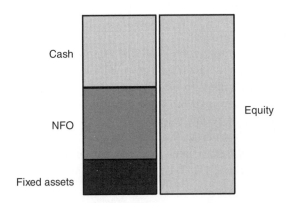

Every company, small or large, high-tech or low, east or west, can have its balance sheet simplified in this way. Cash can of course be on either side of the balance sheet, depending on whether the company has a cash surplus or a credit line. The company's funding might include a long-term loan, which we include as part of the company's capital. As MissInge is a small early stage company, its assets for now are financed with equity.

Look at it this way: companies **only** need cash:

- to invest in property or equipment (fixed assets)
- to cover losses until the company is profitable, to make investments or to pay dividends to shareholders (equity)
- for the items connected with running the business (NFO).

These are the three categories other than surplus cash in our simplified balance sheet. The categories do not change as the company matures, but the use of funding does, whether it is equity from investors or a bank loan/credit line:

- Pre-revenue: buy the company's initial equipment (fixed assets), fund product development and start building the company (losses: a reduction in equity).
- With revenue, but pre-profit: fund losses (equity) and grow sales (NFO).
- With revenue and profits: grow sales (NFO).

As a company becomes more established, NFO becomes increasingly important. A company that remains with very low revenue for longer than expected may have less of a cash problem than a company where sales are taking off faster than planned. Just as you enter a phase when your company is doing well, your investors may negotiate particularly hard to provide new funding; it is a relatively low-risk time for investors to invest, but the company may not have the bandwidth or time to look for alternative funding (a higher NFO means a shorter cash runway).

A semiconductor company, for example, requires huge up-front investment to design and prototype a new silicon chip. All the financing focus at the beginning of the company's life is to get to the point the silicon chip is working and to sign up the first customer. But once the chip works and customer demand takes off, the financing problems have only just started because the NFO may well require an even greater level of funding.

Before we see how NFO relates to the widely used but sometimes confusing expression "Working Capital", we need first to return to Grace and her problems.

Episode 3

Crisis and Confusion

> When you are up to your neck in alligators,
> it is hard to remember the original objective was to drain the swamp.
>
> American proverb

From: Grace Inge
Sent: 11 September 2009 15:07
To: Dan Rossi
Subject: WAY out of my depth

Dan,

I need your help please, Dan. The bank is threatening to foreclose on MissInge – something to do with our balance sheet being skewed, I think, or, as the bank manager put it in his inimitable way, "an alarming rise in assets". What is he on about? A rise in assets, alarming or not, sounds pretty cool to me.

The manager sent me a whole set of financial analyses which I frankly don't understand – I'm not really into numbers, as you know, but if I don't get this fixed in the next couple of weeks the company's toast. The bank manager is serious – that I'm sure about.

I can't go to the board of directors; it would just show them that I'm useless when it comes to numbers and I don't want to give them the satisfaction. They can be pretty smug.

Please send reinforcements or help ASAP!

Grace Inge

CEO
MissInge Fashions

From: Dan Rossi
Sent: 11 September 2009 16:56
To: Grace Inge
Subject: Re: WAY out of my depth

Grace,

I'm your angel shareholder, not your CFO! Let me see if I can find someone to help out. I'll come back to you soonest.

Dan

Chapter 3
NFO and Working Capital

What does your company make?
Award-winning widgets. What does your company make?
Money.

Business joke

Working capital (WC) is the funding available to run the business, hence the name. It is often defined as current assets minus current liabilities. Current assets flow in and out of a company as it conducts its business, including cash, receivables and inventory. Current liabilities are similarly part of the normal business cycle. Payables (purchases of goods and services from suppliers), as well as taxes that have not yet been paid together with any bank credit line are all current liabilities.

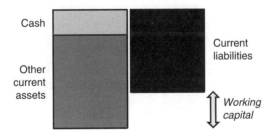

A clearer way of looking at it is the equity minus the fixed assets (because cash is better looked at separately), which is numerically the same thing because it is just the other side of the balance sheet:

Think of it this way: once the fixed assets have been acquired, the remaining funds are available for running the business.

WC increases if equity increases, which happens when profits are made (or there is an equity infusion through an investment or a loan increase). In other words, working capital increases in line with profits.

WC is used to fund items in the top bit of the balance sheet which are concerned with sales, including receivables, inventory and payables, in other words the NFO. NFO and WC might look similar, but there is a key difference.

NFO increases if there is a large amount of inventory, or if customers are slow to pay. It goes down if suppliers provide lots of credit such as long payment terms. So NFO is proportional to sales for so long as payment terms don't change.

If sales go up, so will NFO. If sales double, NFO will broadly double too. It is not precise, not least because some NFO constituents are backward-looking (the receivables are from yesterday's sales) while others are forward looking (inventory is built for tomorrow's sales). So doubling sales may more than double NFO.

The important takeaway is that NFO is broadly proportional to sales, whereas WC is broadly proportional to profits.

WC and NFO are identical when a company has no surplus cash or credit line:

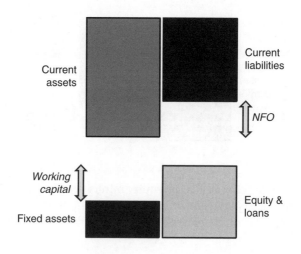

They are very different in what they say about a company. If an announcement is made by a Venture Capital firm that it is investing in a company to "increase its Working Capital", this could mean either that the company is growing so quickly that extra NFO needs financing, or that the company has made losses, reducing the amount of equity available to finance the business. It would be more informative to say "we're investing in NFO" (which means the company is growing) or "we're replenishing the equity" (meaning the company is losing or has lost money).

The difference between the available WC and the NFO is the cash. If there is more WC than NFO, there is surplus cash. If there is less, there needs to be a credit line or some other kind of debt.

Most companies have positive NFO (meaning the NFO needs funding). Here's why: if customers and suppliers each have the same terms of payment with you, the value of receivables will be larger than the payables by the amount of the company's gross margins. If you have any inventory, that just adds to the NFO. As NFO grows with sales, it means that, for most companies, growth needs funding.

Companies with very high gross margins, such as software companies, might be tempted to think this is all a little irrelevant for them. After all, there is no inventory to be financed and none of this old-fashioned making and selling of physical goods. Isn't NFO just for old economy companies?

In fact, software and other tech companies often have particularly high NFO. It's a disadvantage to have no COGS, because suppliers are a great source of funding, and the absence of suppliers means software companies have fewer funding options. Their cost structure consists normally almost entirely of staff. Employees require paying on time every month and will be less tolerant of payment delays than most suppliers would be. Growing software and new media companies is subject to the same NFO rules as conventional companies.

A few companies have negative NFO, such as insurance companies that collect premiums (their sales) before they pay out claims (their COGS). Supermarkets too often receive the cash from selling a product before having to pay the supplier for the item. In these cases more cash is generated the faster the company grows. Supermarkets can use the cash generated from increased sales to build new stores, which fuels further sales growth.

Examples of technology companies with low or negative NFO include SaaS (software as a service) and managed service software companies that typically invoice quarterly or annually in advance.

In fact, invoicing in advance or creating a prepay product is a great way to reduce NFO. More on that later.

Natural cash cycle

As a company carries out its business, buying and selling, paying staff and taxes, the cash balance will vary significantly from day to day. Fluctuating NFO is the reason.

Suppose Grace decided in MissInge's first year to build up inventory for an anticipated spurt in sales at Christmas. If this means that NFO doubles, the balance sheet might look like this before sales start in earnest:

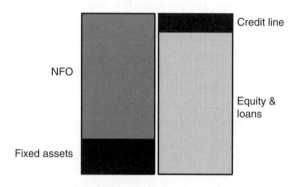

Returning to this, after Christmas is over:

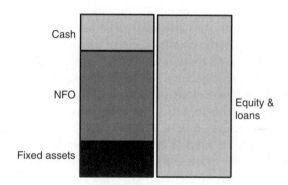

NFO has reduced because the inventory has been sold. Equity has increased from the profits made during the Christmas rush. The changes in each have been enough to move the company from a cash deficit (having a credit line) to having a cash surplus.

Companies need enough cash for the peaks and troughs of this normal cash cycle, so it is important to understand the company's natural cash cycle. As

NFO goes up and down during a day, week, month, quarter and year, it can look like shark teeth when graphed, whereas WC is normally smoother.

The cash cycle includes taxes, which are often paid quarterly or annually in arrears, meaning the cash balance will rise during the quarter and drop when the tax is paid. Many customers only pay bills at the end of the month, so there might be a cash famine during the month followed by a cash feast.

This is an example of a real company that is loss-making, but expecting to reach break-even in about 14 months. Its working capital is falling as the company is making losses, and is then predicted to turn around and increase as the company reaches break-even and becomes profitable. WC is fairly stable being proportional to profits, but the NFO fluctuates during the month as customers typically pay their bills at the end of the month. It also spikes as VAT is paid quarterly (the company in question has few sales outside its national boundaries) and other outgoings are paid quarterly. This graph of the WC and NFO shows the quite distinctive shark-teeth shape of NFO, in line in the short-term with the natural cash cycle of the business, and the smoother line of the WC, which follows profitability:

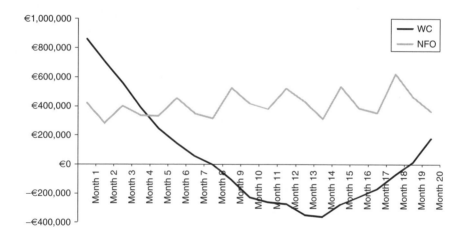

In addition to this natural cycle, NFO is steadily increasing. As NFO is linked to sales, you could (correctly) deduce that the company expects sales to grow.

Most importantly, the company is fast approaching a cash crisis, because WC will be less than NFO in about four months, creating a cash gap. This could be filled by raising money (increasing WC), cutting costs (slowing the decline in WC) or getting better terms from suppliers and customers (reducing NFO).

It would be best to minimize the NFO rather than to raise more equity because that would dilute shareholder returns. It is also preferable to a credit line, as this puts the company at risk if the credit is withdrawn. A credit facility is also likely to be expensive.

What this graph does not show is that the company has an invoicing discounting facility of €500,000 which it is not yet using, so in fact the company will not run out of cash until month 9.

(There is a postscript on this company: it did indeed reach a cash crisis nine months later and was not able to pay its VAT bill. After discussions with the existing investors who were reluctant to invest further funds, the company was sold to a trade buyer for a knock-down price.)

It is often helpful to visualize the cash movements. This is an example of the cash balance of a company that buys a product for €80 and sells it for €100 (the elapsed days are taken from a real example). The product is held in inventory on average for 36 days before it is sold. The customer pays on average 15 days later on day 51. The supplier is then paid on day 132, meaning the company has the use of the cash for about 80 days. This is a graph of the cash situation in connection with that transaction:

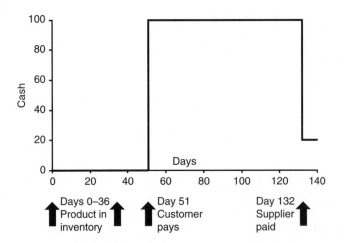

The graph finishes at 20, being the profit made from the sale. The area under the graph, being a combination of time and cash, is equivalent to the NFO. As the cash balance is always positive in this example of Company A, the NFO is negative. This means the company is getting a lot of free operational financing from its suppliers.

This is another company selling the same product that it buys for €80 and sells for €100. It also holds the product in inventory for 36 days. Being a small company, it has to pay its suppliers in 30 days, while its customers pay in 60 days. This is the graph of the cash:

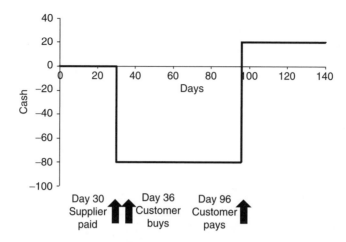

So to secure the €20 profit from this sale, Company B has to invest €80 for 66 days.

NFO is tightly linked to the speed a company can grow. In fact they are not just tightly linked; NFO determines the speed a company can grow without additional external funding, as we will see.

Episode 4

Grace gets Some Help

Curiouser and curiouser!

Lewis Carroll

From: Dan Rossi
Sent: 16 September 2009 11:03
To: Grace Inge
Subject: Re: WAY out of my depth

Grace,

I've found someone to help you. He is brilliant with numbers and can explain everything to you. But you are going to have to go centre-stage on this one – he's just not the type you can put in front of a bank or investors; he's more of a backroom boy. He does numbers, not people.

It will be a good opportunity for you really to get to grips with the company's finances – it's about time you learned their importance!

I'll make the introduction by separate email and leave you to sort out fees etc. with him. I don't believe he'll be that expensive.

Keep in touch, Grace. These are interesting times.

Dan

From: Grace Inge
Sent: 16 September 2009 15:01
To: Dan Rossi
Subject: Re: WAY out of my depth

Dan,

Where do you find these people? Anyway, he and I have spoken and agreed terms. He has already started asking lots of questions, which is good, because if I under-stand the question I feel I have a better chance of understanding the answer. If only balance sheets had been an optional module at design school (except I probably wouldn't have taken it)!

Dan, you're a star and I owe you big time. Dinner's on me next time.

Grace Inge

CEO
MissInge Fashions

Chapter 4
Growing As Fast As Possible without New Investment

Make the iron hot by striking it.

Oliver Cromwell

Sustainable growth (defined as growing as fast as possible without additional financing) is achieved by making sure NFO growth does not exceed the profits generated. The formula for sustainable growth is very simple:

$$\text{sustainable growth rate} = \frac{\text{profitability}}{\text{NFO as \% of sales}}$$

The reason for this can be easily deduced. Assuming the way the company does business doesn't change, NFO is a fixed percentage of sales, or

$$\text{NFO} = n * \text{sales}$$

Where n is the NFO percentage. If sales change, NFO will change proportionately:

$$\Delta\text{NFO} = n * \Delta\text{sales}$$

Working capital increases as profits are made, which is the same as sales times return on sales (ROS):

$$\Delta\text{WC} = \text{net income} = \text{ROS} * \text{sales}$$

The maximum growth a company can sustain is when the increase in NFO equals the net income, so:

$$\Delta\text{NFO} = \Delta\text{WC}$$

Putting the two formulae together, we get:

n * Δsales = ROS * sales

So the sustainable growth rate "g" is:

$$g = \frac{\Delta sales}{S} = \frac{ROS}{n}$$

So sustainable growth is the profitability divided by the NFO as a percentage of sales.

This might all be a bit theoretical for an entrepreneur, but it means that a company's growth does not necessarily need to be funded by a bank facility; it could instead be financed by reducing NFO, increasing profits or by slowing down growth. And it can easily be calculated.

Suppose your company's profit, its net income, is 10 per cent of sales. With a very high NFO of 50 per cent of sales, the company could only grow at 20 per cent per year without running out of cash (g = 10%/50% = 20%). On the other hand it would be able to double sales if NFO were 10 per cent of sales (g = 10%/10% = 100%).

The formula works for either absolute amounts or as a percentage of sales.

The best way to understand how to use this is to go back to our story of Grace at MissInge.

Grace's initial plan for MissInge was to start by selling other companies' clothes, with a focus on jackets. She would carefully select the products from high-quality, unknown companies and put her name on them. That way she could build the brand of MissInge and set out to design her own range, which would require external funding. She plans in the first year of trading to have sales of €180,000 and to make a small profit of €10,000. MissInge's NFO is (as we know from earlier) 11 per cent of sales. Her NFO in monetary terms is therefore the sales of 180 * 11%, or €19,800. Therefore:

$$\text{sustainable growth rate } = \frac{€10k}{€19.8k} = 50\%$$

Sales in the second year could therefore be 50 per cent higher, or a total of €270,000, without needing additional funding.

This can equally well be calculated using percentages: NFO is 11 per cent and profitability is 5.5 per cent return on sales. The sustainable growth rate is therefore:

$$\text{sustainable growth rate} = \frac{5.5\%}{11\%} = 50\%$$

NFO can be quite large in some companies. A software company that is paid royalties 4.5 months after the product is delivered (this would be typical for a company paid quarterly in arrears) would have an NFO of 4.5/12, or 37.5 per cent. If it has MissInge's profits of 5.5 per cent of sales, it only has funding to grow at 15 per cent per year. Ouch.

The relationship between NFO and the sustainable growth rate is not linear, because if there is no NFO, growth can theoretically be infinite (in reality, companies would need for example to buy fixed assets as they grow). On the other hand, if NFO is infinite there can be no growth. The point beyond the rather theoretical arithmetic is that a small change in reducing NFO can materially improve a company's ability to grow. So it is worth making an effort to achieve even a small reduction in NFO. Here is the graph of the relationship for a company with 10 per cent profitability:

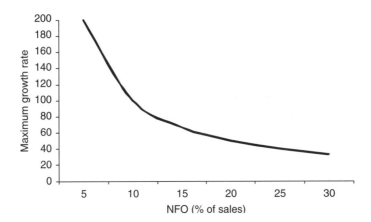

Of course, many start-up companies do not generate profits, so the formula for the sustainable growth rate of profitability divided by NFO does not work. The principles remain the same though, and sustainable sales growth can be calculated for entrepreneurial companies, profitable or not. It is even possible to work out when the next round of funding is needed.

Calculating sustainable growth

First, the NFO is calculated by looking at the balance sheet. The main elements of NFO are the accounts receivable, inventory and accounts payable, but pre-payments, accruals and deferred revenue should be included, if there are any.

Calculate the NFO in terms of the percentage of sales to be financed. For Grace in her first year of operations it looked like this:

Inventory: 30 days of sales, or about 8 per cent of sales

Receivables: 30 days of sales, or about 8 per cent of sales

Payables: 20 days of sales, or about 5 per cent of sales

This corresponds to an NFO of 40 days of sales (30 days of inventory plus 30 days of receivables minus 20 days of payables), or 11 per cent of annual sales.

These figures should be checked against the balance sheet. (Inventory figures in particular can often be underestimated – it is natural to forget slow-moving or obsolete stock!) Necessary cash needs to be calculated by estimating the peaks and troughs of the NFO – this is the cash included in NFO because it is needed for the operations. The best way to do this is to look at balance sheets from previous periods to see how much the NFO varies from month to month. Alternatively, add a month. (Most bills and expenses are paid monthly so this may be a reasonable approximation of the difference between the NFO peak and trough.)

You can alternatively estimate your NFO by drawing a timeline, showing when you buy components from suppliers, how long it takes to build and ship products, and when you will be paid. This is a particularly good technique for new products, as the business around each product has its own NFO.

After you have completed this analysis, you should have a pretty accurate view of the company's NFO. Let's assume you have arrived at a figure of 25 per cent of annual sales. This means that for every additional €1 of sales, you need 25 cents of funding. Remember that NFO is the sum of all the company's cash movements for selling, expressed as a percentage of annual sales. Most businesses sell a mix of products and changing the mix may well change the NFO and the company's cash flow.

If you divide your company's surplus cash by the NFO you have calculated, you will have the amount of additional sales the company can support with its current level of cash. If sales are currently €5 million, your NFO is 25% and there is €1 million of surplus cash, you could add €4 million of sales (€1 million/0.25) to take sales to €9 million.

You can now project this forwards into future years by adjusting for anticipated losses or profits as well as any fixed assets you need to buy. Suppose you expect the company to make losses this year of €300,000, €200,000 next year and to be break-even thereafter, on sales of €7 million next year and €11 million the year after. You also need to increase fixed assets by €100,000 each year net of depreciation.

The best way is to construct a simple Balance Sheet:

	This year	Year +1	Year +2
Sales	€5,000k	€7,000k	€11,000k
Profit	−€200k	−€100k	€0k
Equity	€2,350k	€2,250k	€2,250k
NFO 25%	€1,250k	€1,750k	€2,750k
Fixed assets	€100k	€200k	€300k
Assets	€1,350k	€1,950k	€3,050k
Cash to balance	€1,000k	€300k	−€800k

The losses this year and next reduce the equity. The NFO increases in line with sales and, together with the assets, represent the items that need funding. Surplus cash and equity provide the funding.

The company will run out of cash early in year 2, when it will need another round of finance.

So, armed with the NFO estimate, the company's sales and profit projections and the amount planned to spend on buying assets, the timing of the next financing round can be calculated. At that point the company has the option, as an alternative to additional financing, to stop growing or at least to slow down. This will stop the NFO rising and the company can cruise along. It is always preferable not to be under too much time pressure when raising money!

Working out how much cash is needed is even possible before the company starts trading. First calculate the NFO as a percentage of sales, to be able to say, "for every €1,000 of sales, we need €x in cash". This is the variable amount of funding needed.

Then calculate and add together all the operating losses before the company expects to be profitable (you probably have this figure in your P&L business plan) and list all the assets that are needed for the operation of the company. This is the start-up funding.

The amount of cash your company needs to any particular point in time is therefore:

cash need = start-up funding + (sales * variable funding), or

cash need = fixed assets + losses until break-even + (sales * NFO)

This model is imperfect in that the cash needs from losses may peak at a different time to those from NFO. The three (fixed assets, losses and NFO) added together form the famous cash "J curve" of start-ups, with the trough of the

J curve being the point where cash is cumulatively at its lowest point. But it remains a great way to carry out some scenario planning or stress-testing of the company. What would happen if sales are later than anticipated, or sales grow more quickly? Try some different scenarios to make sure the company is adequately funded under all likely situations. Having a good grasp of what affects cash in your business is the first step to being able to control it.

Think of it this way: if cash is the gas, growth is a gas guzzler. But you don't necessarily need to drive more slowly; you just need to learn to drive more economically.

Episode 5

The Bank Helps

The nine most terrifying words in the English language are, "I'm from the government and I'm here to help."

Ronald Reagan

Though they are quite different, Grace quite likes Hans. He is earnest, generally unsmiling and can't stop pressing his gold-rimmed glasses back up his nose. Everything about him epitomizes "bank manager", from his grey suit to his light-blue shirt and boring tie. Grace and Hans are about the same age, but seem to come from different planets.

Grace wonders what he thinks of her, with her large smile, loud laugh, permanently windswept hair, expensive taste in shoes and her famous-name leather bag overflowing with the detritus from her personal and business lives.

But just occasionally, she feels she gets through to him. There is a sparkle in his eye, or the hint of a smile on his thin lips. She once saw a press cutting of her receiving an award sitting in his in-tray and she suspects that he is quite proud to have this mini-celebrity as his client.

So was he serious about shutting MissInge down? Hans does not really ever joke and certainly not about anything as serious as balance sheets. Grace decides to start the meeting with some levity.

"Don't ever do that to me again, Hans."

"Don't ever do what, Grace?"

"Call me up when I'm about to get an award and tell me that MissInge is going to be shut down."

"That is still very much on the cards, I'm afraid. I have a brief reprieve from regional office to find a solution, but only with a lot of string-pulling. Let's see where we get to in this meeting and hopefully we can save MissInge."

Grace looks disappointed at her failed attempt at levity. Hans seems to smile in recognition of the moment.

"So let's get going. Here's the analysis prepared by the bank," says Hans, back behind his business veil as he hands out PowerPoint slides.

"MissInge Fashions' prospects look really good, even if the company is still unprofitable. We all knew that this year and last were going to be periods of investment, which is why you raised €4 million in equity and a €0.5 million facility from us. The investment in sales and marketing is really starting to pay off, with strong sales growth in the current year. Next year in 2010 you expect – for good reason I understand – sales to grow even faster and to show a small profit at the EBITDA level at least. This growth is expected to continue for the foreseeable future, at least for as long as the current planning horizon. This first slide shows the P&L development over the years."

MissInge Fashions, P&L

The bank for entrepreneurs

P&L in €000		Recent Years			Forecast			
		2007	2008	2009	2010	2011	2012	2013
Sales	(1)	180	1,350	2,592	10,653	16,022	19,373	23,248
Raw material Microfibre		-65	-473	-855	-3,409	-4,807	-5,812	-6,974
Raw material others		-41	-305	-570	-2,301	-3,365	-4,068	-4,882
Manufacturing		-27	-203	-311	-1,087	-1,634	-1,976	-2,371
shipping (percentage of sales) [2.8%]		-5	-38	-73	-298	-449	-542	-651
Gross margin		42	332	783	3,558	5,768	6,974	8,369
Personnel costs	(2)	-280	-560	-2,170	-2,520	-3,080	-3,430	-4,130
Operating costs as % of Headcount [40%]	(3)	-112	-224	-868	-1,008	-1,232	-1,372	-1,652
EBITDA		-350	-452	-2,255	30	1,456	2,172	2,587
Depreciation [25%]	(4)	0	-5	-34	-518	-963	-957	-865
EBIT		-350	-457	-2,289	-488	493	1,215	1,723
Financial expenses net [13%]	(5)	0	0	0	0	-460	-664	-677
EBT		-350	-457	-2,289	-488	33	551	1,045
GM %		23%	25%	30%	33%	36%	36%	36%

"Your gross margin is improving as volumes increase and your expenses are not expected to grow as quickly as sales, and as a result there is good profit growth."

"If you achieve these numbers, you will dramatically change the company over the next three years: the company will be ten times bigger and be generating good and consistent profits. This all seems a very attractive proposition. The losses will shortly be behind you and the future suggests both good growth and consistent profits."

"So what's the problem?" asks Grace.

"Just to be clear, Grace, I accept these numbers. I think you have a very good chance of achieving them. It's the financial structure of the company that is causing me concern. Slide two please. This is a graph of your forecast profit, taken from the figures we looked at in the previous slide."

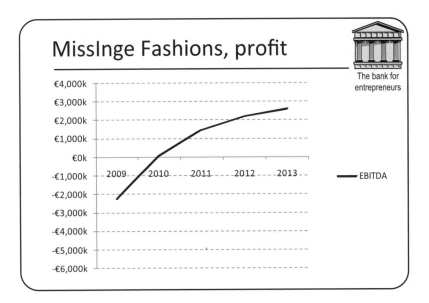

"It's just sometimes easier to understand figures from a graph. Let's place our closing cash balance estimate on this graph as well. Grace, we are not comfortable with your cash flow forecasts, so these are the bank's own estimates."

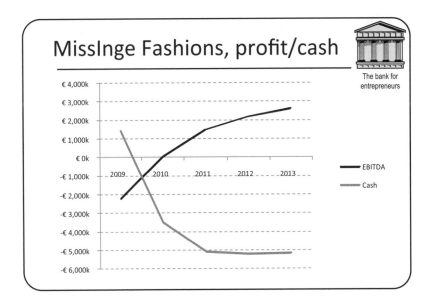

"How can that possibly be right?" asks Grace, perplexed. "There is no way we need over €5 million, surely?"

"Actually, I believe you may need more than €5 million, but let's take this a step at a time," replies Hans. "It just takes too long between your paying to make the jackets and receiving the cash from the customer, distributor or shop. It's made worse particularly by manufacturing in China and shipping the goods by sea."

"But it's just too expensive to use air freight."

"I understand why you freight by sea, but it does make your cash situation worse. Let's come back to that in a moment; I want to go into more detail about the cash needs of the company, starting with the product manufacturing costs. Next slide, please."

MissInge Fashions - COGS

The bank for entrepreneurs

	€	€	
Typical retail price		99.00	
ex-VAT (average 20%)		82.50	
Sale price by MissInge		41.25	100%
Labour	4.21		10%
Microfibre	13.20		32%
Components, packaging	8.91		22%
Shipping	1.16		2.8%
Total COGS		27.47	67%
Gross profit		13.78	33%

"The jackets sell for an average of €99 and you give up about 50 per cent in margin into the resellers and distributors. That means you receive about €41 per jacket, which costs about €27 to make, giving an average gross margin of 33 per cent. The margin is also improving as manufacturing volumes increase." Hans is in full flow.

"That feels right," says Grace.

"MissInge designs its products in Italy and manufactures in China in order to improve margins. Labour costs are about 10 per cent of the cost of the jacket. MissInge estimates that labour costs in China are about a quarter those of Europe, and with Gross Margins of 35 per cent, manufacturing in Europe would consume all your profits."

"Yes, that's why we manufacture in China," agrees Grace.

"I note that the main component of the jacket, the microfibre, is bought from the manufacturer in Europe, who then ships it to your factory in

China directly. As MissInge is small and unprofitable, when the relationship started the supplier insisted on MissInge paying for the fabric in advance."

"They still do, but I'm working on that," says Grace defensively.

"Isn't the microfibre made in Asia somewhere?" asks Hans.

"Actually I think the material is made in China too. I've asked the supplier why it takes so long between our paying and the microfibre being delivered to our factory but they tell me that's just the way it is. I don't think we're really a big enough customer for them to make an effort to be honest. It's a pain but it's something we have learned to live with."

"I understand – that sort of thing is one of the problems of being a small company," Hans continues, "but let me move on. The jackets are too heavy to send economically by air, so they are normally on the high seas for four to six weeks en route to MissInge's warehouse before being shipped to the retailer. The retailers typically settle the invoices 60 days from receipt of goods. To understand how much cash MissInge needs, we need to look at each step in the manufacturing of a jacket, how long it takes and what it costs. Next slide, please. These are the key timings."

Manufacturing timing

The bank for entrepreneurs

	Days	Total
Microfibre received and paid for	0	0
Microfibre shipment time to China	15	15
Jacket manufacturing time	45	60
Shipping time to EU warehouse	45	105
Average time in warehouse	15	120
Average customer payment	60	180

"As you can see, we estimate about two weeks to get the microfibre to the factory. It then takes about six weeks to manufacture the jacket. This seems a long time, but we understand the various suppliers are only prepared to deliver monthly, so there is quite a lot of component inventory. In order to save money on shipping costs, shipments to the warehouse in Europe are only made monthly as well. So 45 days is in fact quite quick."

"Shipping from Shanghai to Europe takes another 45 days on average, including the time it takes to get the jackets through customs and into the warehouse. The jackets on average spend only two weeks in your warehouse in Europe, which is excellent, but bearing in mind you only receive a delivery from China once a month, it means you are often short of stock."

Grace frowns because Hans is right. MissInge seems to be permanently out of stock and she spends a lot of time trying to work out which customer to supply. This has led to some disgruntled resellers in particular. She decides not to interrupt Hans.

"Then," Hans continues, "as we discussed, the customers pay in about 60 days. I know you are selling more and more from your website, getting the cash instantly from the credit card companies, but that is offset by increased international sales, where payment is often delayed because your distributors pay more slowly than shops, which is perhaps understandable as they would prefer to be paid by their customers before they pay you."

"The total manufacturing and payment cycle is therefore 180 days. A good way of looking at it is by using a timeline. Next slide, please."

"All in all, it takes about six months from ordering and paying for the microfibre until you are paid by your customer," Hans explains.

"Wow, that's long. But I get it."

"OK," Hans continues, "the best way to work out what funding is required is by forecasting a balance sheet from the P&L we looked at earlier. Next slide, please."

Financial drivers

The bank for entrepreneurs

Drivers		2007	2008	2009	2010	2011	2012	2013
Sales growth	(%)		650%	92%	311%	50%	21%	20%
Raw Material: Microfibre as % sales	(%)	36%	35%	33%	32%	30%	30%	30%
Raw Material: other as % sales	(%)	23%	23%	22%	22%	21%	21%	21%
Manufacturing as % sales	(%)	15%	15%	12%	10%	10%	10%	10%
Capex in €	(Euro)	20	120	1,970	2,300	940	586	678
Accounts receivable	(days)	60	60	60	60	60	60	60
Days of Raw Material Microfibre	(days)	33	33	33	33	33	33	33
Days of inventory finished goods	(days)	75	75	75	75	75	75	75
Account payables Microfibre	(days)	0	0	0	0	0	0	0

"We start with the financial drivers of the business, the things that can affect the P&L and the balance sheet. The sales growth is just the figure from the P&L we looked at earlier."

"The raw materials and manufacturing percentages affect the Cost of Goods Sold line in the P&L. You can see the planned improvement in margin as volumes increase."

"The capex line item represents the capital assets you plan to acquire. We've talked about this at length at the time of the last funding round, but your focus this year is to invest in equipment for your European warehouse and next year to buy production machinery to increase production in China. Capex affects the balance sheet."

"The remaining items: accounts receivable, the days the microfibre and finished goods are held in inventory and the accounts payable all also affect the balance sheet."

"Let's start by looking at the assets side of the balance sheet. Next slide, please."

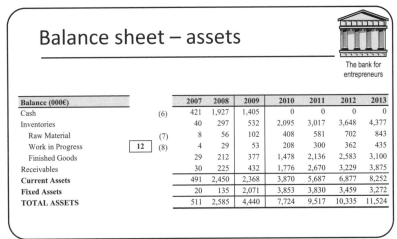

Balance sheet – assets

The bank for entrepreneurs

Balance (000€)			2007	2008	2009	2010	2011	2012	2013
Cash		(6)	421	1,927	1,405	0	0	0	0
Inventories			40	297	532	2,095	3,017	3,648	4,377
Raw Material		(7)	8	56	102	408	581	702	843
Work in Progress	12	(8)	4	29	53	208	300	362	435
Finished Goods			29	212	377	1,478	2,136	2,583	3,100
Receivables			30	225	432	1,776	2,670	3,229	3,875
Current Assets			491	2,450	2,368	3,870	5,687	6,877	8,252
Fixed Assets			20	135	2,071	3,853	3,830	3,459	3,272
TOTAL ASSETS			511	2,585	4,440	7,724	9,517	10,335	11,524

"Let me explain this line by line," says Hans. "You can see immediately my concern over cash. Even with the two million additional euros from the investors, that completely disappears very soon and, as we will see when we look at the liabilities, you end up with a large cash hole."

"All these figures assume the full €4 million investment is paid into the company by the way," Hans explains.

"We have broken inventory into raw material, which is mainly the micro-fibre; work in progress which, at 12 days, is a very small component of the 180-day cycle of financing making and selling the product, and finished goods, which represents the completed jackets. Is that clear?" asks Hans.

"I don't understand how we have such large inventories of finished goods when we appear to be out of stock the whole time," says Grace.

"Well, that's because most of the time the finished jackets are being shipped from China rather than sitting in your warehouse. They still count as finished goods," explains Hans.

Grace nods slowly. "I understand."

"Inventories and receivables are growing because your sales are growing. This is what I meant by an alarming rise in assets – all of which need funding."

"Funding?"

"Balance sheets always balance, so if assets are rising there must be an equal rise in liabilities and equity. In other words your suppliers, investors or us, the bank, need to provide the funding for the increase in assets." Hans waits for Grace to absorb what he has said.

"I think I understand. Can we look at the other side of the balance sheet?" asks Grace.

"OK. Next slide, please."

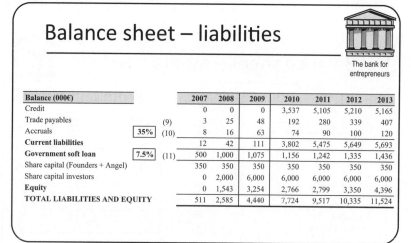

Balance sheet – liabilities

The bank for entrepreneurs

Balance (000€)			2007	2008	2009	2010	2011	2012	2013
Credit			0	0	0	3,537	5,105	5,210	5,165
Trade payables		(9)	3	25	48	192	280	339	407
Accruals	35%	(10)	8	16	63	74	90	100	120
Current liabilities			12	42	111	3,802	5,475	5,649	5,693
Government soft loan	7.5%	(11)	500	1,000	1,075	1,156	1,242	1,335	1,436
Share capital (Founders + Angel)			350	350	350	350	350	350	350
Share capital investors			0	2,000	6,000	6,000	6,000	6,000	6,000
Equity			0	1,543	3,254	2,766	2,799	3,350	4,396
TOTAL LIABILITIES AND EQUITY			511	2,585	4,440	7,724	9,517	10,335	11,524

"Let me explain it again line by line," says Hans. "The credit line item is the cash debt you would have if things are left the way they are."

"Should I think of it as the balancing item?" asks Grace.

"Yes, that's right – whatever the gap is between the assets that need funding and the liabilities and equity that provide the funding must be covered by cash. To carry on down the various items, the trade payables are the sum of all the unpaid supplier invoices."

"The amounts are pretty small," comments Grace.

"I agree. Remember these liabilities are sources of funding, in that they enable you to finance the assets. Part of MissInge's financial problem is that your suppliers are not providing you with much credit."

Hans pauses to look at the grim-faced Grace.

"Hmmm. And what are the accruals?" asks Grace, looking up.

"Almost entirely payroll taxes not due for payment until next month. They run at about 35 per cent of your monthly salary bill."

"I see."

"For the soft loan you got from the government agency, I have assumed you will not actually pay the interest, is that right?" asks Hans.

"There is 7.5 per cent interest to be paid every year, but they are pretty flexible about not demanding payment if we can't afford it, in which case it just gets added to the loan we owe."

"Yes, that's what we assumed," answers Hans, "so we allowed for the interest payments to compound and for the loan just to keep growing. The share capital line items show the €350,000 invested by you and Mr Rossi and the €6 million from the VCs."

"Where does the equity line item come from? It doesn't seem to fit into anything," asks Grace.

"It's the sum of all your profits plus the share capital. Up to the end of last year, for example, you had made total losses of €807,000. Subtracting that from the €2.35 million of share capital gets you the €1,543 equity figure."

"Is everything clear? Because I would like to move on if it is," asks Hans.

"Yes, please continue."

"We have calculated MissInge's Necessary Funds for Operations – its NFO – from the balance sheet. It is simply the inventory plus the receivables minus the payables and the accruals. So taking the figures from the current year 2009, we add together the inventory figure of €532,000 and the receivables of €432,000, less the payables of €48,000 and the accruals of €63,000, making an NFO of €853,000. Dividing that into the revenue of €2,593,000 gives an NFO 33 per cent."

"The two largest offenders are the inventory and the accounts receivable – they make up the bulk of the NFO."

"So what you are saying if I understand you correctly is that every time we increase sales by €1 we need another 33 cents of funding? That just seems enormous," complains Grace.

"It may in fact be conservative; there are also the fixed assets that need financing. This calculation also ignores the effect of VAT, which can make a significant difference to some businesses. If VAT has to be paid to the government before the cash is received from the customer, or VAT is paid from a supplier and the sale is exempt from VAT, it can have an important effect on cash flow, in which case this too will need to be modelled. We decided there were other more important issues, but you might like to have a look at that yourself when you have a moment."

"The NFO may also be larger in 2009 and 2010 than this model shows, because the company is growing so quickly. This means that the inventory is being built for tomorrow's sales, which are significantly higher, rather than today's. Sales are growing at up to 50 per cent a quarter, so with such a long manufacturing and inventory cycle, each manufacturing cycle is 50 per cent bigger than the last, but is being funded by yesterday's sales."

Grace is too stunned to say anything and she just raises an eyebrow. Hans continues.

"The balance sheet can be simplified into the items that need financing and those that provide financing. Look at this slide," says Hans.

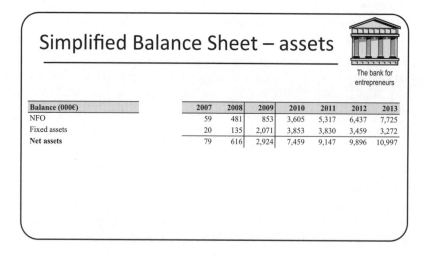

Simplified Balance Sheet – assets

The bank for entrepreneurs

Balance (000€)	2007	2008	2009	2010	2011	2012	2013
NFO	59	481	853	3,605	5,317	6,437	7,725
Fixed assets	20	135	2,071	3,853	3,830	3,459	3,272
Net assets	79	616	2,924	7,459	9,147	9,896	10,997

"These are the items that need funding and, as you can see, there is tremendous growth for many years to come. The sources of funding just can't keep up – let me show you. Next slide, please."

Simplified Balance Sheet

The bank for entrepreneurs

Balance (000€)	2007	2008	2009	2010	2011	2012	2013
NFO	59	481	853	3,605	5,317	6,437	7,725
Fixed assets	20	135	2,071	3,853	3,830	3,459	3,272
Net assets	79	616	2,924	7,459	9,147	9,896	10,997
Long Term Debt	500	1,000	1,075	1,156	1,242	1,335	1,436
Equity	0	1,543	3,254	2,766	2,799	3,350	4,396
Financing	500	2,543	4,329	3,922	4,041	4,686	5,831
Cash surplus (+), Credit (-)	421	1,927	1,405	-3,537	-5,105	-5,210	-5,165
Cash generated per year	421	1,506	-523	-4,941	-1,568	-105	45

"The sources of funding come from the debt, which is growing because you are accruing but not paying the interest, and the equity, which is where profits end up. The bottom line shows that this year, and for the next three, the company is going to continue to consume lots of cash," concludes Hans.

After a pause, Hans says, "There's another thing I need to mention, that makes the matter even worse, I'm afraid."

"What's that?" asks Grace a little nervously.

"I don't believe your sales forecasts. It's not that they are too high, but that they might very well be too low. As you now realize, being too high is worse than being too low for the purposes of your cash flow."

"Why don't you believe them?" Grace asks.

"You are predicting growth to slow quite dramatically, from tripling next year to 50 per cent the year after and down to 20 per cent after that. It just looks a little too neat."

"So I asked Joe, your head of sales, about forecasting. He joked that, 'Long-term planning for me is working out what we will sell next quarter.' In other words he can't see beyond the manufacturing horizon."

"He was always one to shoot his mouth off," grumbles Grace.

"We know that the warehouse is often out of stock," continues Hans, "so there is some unfulfilled demand. You are expanding rapidly overseas yet you still forecast most of the sales will come from the domestic market. There is also so much publicity around you, the company and the Carrera jacket that will keep stoking sales demand."

"I never thought I'd hear a bank tell me my sales forecasts are too low."

Hans doesn't react and instead keeps going.

"If I am right that your sales forecasts are conservative, your cash situation will be even worse. With a high NFO we know that MissInge will need more cash, but how much? The answer is lots. We've run the numbers with a 75 per cent annual growth rate, a figure that Joe thinks is quite possible, possibly even conservative. It produces an eye-wateringly attractive P&L. Next slide, please."

P&L forecast w/ 75% growth

The bank for entrepreneurs

P&L in €000			Recent Years			Forecast			
			2007	2008	2009	2010	2011	2012	2013
Sales		(1)	180	1,350	2,592	10,653	18,643	32,625	57,094
Raw material Microfibre			-65	-473	-855	-3,409	-5,593	-9,788	-17,128
Raw material others			-41	-305	-570	-2,301	-3,915	-6,851	-11,990
Manufacturing			-27	-203	-311	-1,087	-1,902	-3,328	-5,824
shipping (percentage of sales)	2.8%		-5	-38	-73	-298	-522	-914	-1,599
Gross margin			42	332	783	3,558	6,711	11,745	20,554
Personnel costs		(2)	-280	-560	-2,170	-2,520	-3,584	-5,776	-10,143
Operating costs as % of Headcount	40%	(3)	-112	-224	-868	-1,008	-1,434	-2,311	-4,057
EBITDA			-350	-452	-2,255	30	1,694	3,658	6,354
Depreciation	25%	(4)	0	-5	-34	-518	-963	-1,072	-1,416
EBIT			-350	-457	-2,289	-488	731	2,586	4,938
Financial expenses net	13%	(5)	0	0	0	0	-460	-805	-1,346
EBT			-350	-457	-2,289	-488	271	1,781	3,593

"I have assumed that your personnel costs rise in proportion to revenue, which is quite cautious. Even so, you can see that in four years MissInge would have sales of €57 million and EBITDA of over €6 million."

"Well I think it is quite possible to grow like that; it just seems a little over-optimistic to plan that much growth," says Grace.

"Companies with a high NFO need to model high sales growth, because you need to work out how much cash you would need. In this case, unfortunately, your cash requirement would be over €15 million. We've plotted our cash estimates against the estimates from your current plan. Slide please."

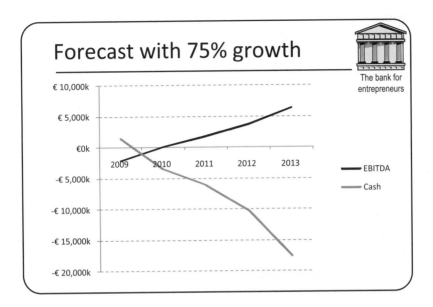

"Look at the cash line, Grace. You can see the rate at which your company is bleeding cash and there is no sign of it stopping," Hans continues.

"You need to finance tomorrow's sales with cash from yesterday's profits, so the company would not be cash generative until either profits improve as a percentage of sales, or NFO improves or growth slows. And that is despite the excellent P&L," explains Hans.

"It is quite likely," he continues, "that MissInge will continue to need cash every year for the foreseeable future. Cash generated from the previous year's profit will be more than absorbed in increased NFO and the very considerable capital investments you need to make every time you add new production line capacity in China."

"But If I slow growth down, I will lose the momentum I have with the market. So that's not an option."

"I understand, Grace, but the whole future of the company is at stake as we speak. Before we break, let me give you a simple formula that might help," suggests Hans helpfully.

"The sustainable growth rate is your profitability divided by your NFO. With profits, for example, of 3 per cent and an NFO of 33 per cent, you can only fund sales growth of 10 per cent per year. If profits rise to 6 per cent, the sales growth can increase to 20 per cent. Here's a simple formula to check whether MissInge will generate or consume cash." Hans walks to the white-board and starts writing:

cash generative: if profit > NFO x sales growth

cash consuming: if profit < NFO x sales growth

"Let me suggest you go away and think how to improve your profit or lower the NFO. I think you will get a larger effect if you focus on NFO," suggests Hans. "Don't forget to include any fixed assets which you may need in addition to the NFO."

"That will only make matters worse!" complains Grace. "Can I have your model to help me?"

"Of course. Here's a copy of the presentation and I will email you the workings." Hans hands over a neat dossier of papers to Grace.

"We've included all the investments you plan and it shows how we get to the cash needs of the company. Let's meet again once you have a plan, Grace. My main message is that no bank is going to lend to a company with a large and ever-growing NFO. It's an old saying, but for you, Grace, it is more than relevant. Cash really is king."

Chapter 5
Building a Cash-lean Company

If you're going through hell, keep going.

Winston Churchill

There is a general trend for larger companies to require longer supplier payment terms (even some supermarkets, which really don't need the cash, are paying more slowly). Although the picture varies from country to country, there appears to be a general drift to paying at the end of the month rather than the agreed number of days from the invoice, and 30 days payment is increasingly being replaced by 60, 90 days or even longer. Wherever you look, country or industry, the trend is in the wrong direction. What started out as giving the customer enough time to process payments has ended up as the customer using suppliers as a source of funding.

This is a major problem for a start-up, where cash is king.

Large companies are lengthening payment terms to reduce their own NFO, thus receiving free funding. But for a start-up, funding locked up in NFO is not available to be spent on other things a start-up would like to spend it on, such as fixed assets, sales and marketing expansion and product development. In other words delaying payment stifles innovation. So everyone loses.

The right thing for customers to do would in fact be to offer to pay earlier, in exchange perhaps for a discount. But let's stop dreaming; it is up to the entrepreneur to find a solution to this.

Every company should try to minimize its NFO. Getting your customers and suppliers to finance your company is the cheapest source of capital around, as well as the most reliable and consistent. It can also generally be done without upsetting relationships, or reducing profitability. Reducing NFO can in some cases make the difference between survival and bankruptcy, whether a start-up can grow fast enough as the market takes off and ultimately whether the founders of the business make a return from their investment and hard work.

It's tempting just to say that NFO should be funded by a credit line. But credit lines are not easy to get for an entrepreneurial company with a short

51

and perhaps unprofitable history. Banks look for security on their loans and the accounts receivable are the best security. Banks prefer to lend to companies that sell domestically because it is harder to recover money from customers in other countries, perhaps with additional risks such as exchange rates. As an example, this is an extract from a letter sent by a bank to a small, fast-growing company:

> "*Regretfully, I will not be able to put an overdraft facility at your disposal over the coming weeks... Notwithstanding the quality of the debtor book, many are based overseas... The bank therefore places a very limited reliance on its ability to collect... all I can suggest is that you continue to manipulate your cash flow within the bounds of cash received, in order to maintain a credit balance on the bank account.*"

The trick is to reduce NFO rather than getting a credit line. Doing so requires some leadership from you, the entrepreneur, and some changes in the way your company works internally, particularly in product management. The improvement can be dramatic and surprising.

Lead from the top

Cash may indeed be king, but the chances are the management report you look at starts with sales orders. To instil the importance of cash to the company, cash-related metrics need to be one of the company's top Key Performance Indicators (KPIs).

The old saying "You don't get what you expect, you get what you inspect" works well here. Include an NFO report in the standard management information pack that goes to the senior management team. Set NFO-related KPIs and tie bonuses to their achievement. For example, many companies reward CFOs on the basis of Free Cash Flow, but this does not take into account sales growth, which should be encouraged provided it is sustainable. A better KPI is probably "NFO as a percentage of sales", or just plain NFO. If this is tracked every month you will be able to see what kind of natural cycle it has. This is best in the form of a graph. (One of the plus points is that VCs and many accountants are not familiar with the full beauty of NFO, so you will have the kudos of explaining it to them!)

An alternative more classic cash KPI is DSO (Days Sales Outstanding) but this only considers cash tied up in receivables. It works best for software companies and others that have little inventory.

Many management reports and budgets do not include balance sheets which are arguably the most important financial instrument. Graphing is a particularly powerful way of seeing what is going on within a balance sheet and including a cash and NFO graph in the Business Plan will ensure that NFO is being planned and optimized up-front.

The management report should also include a cash flow forecast for at least 13 weeks or as long as the cash cycle lasts. As mentioned before, NFO's natural cycle is likely to be over one quarter to allow for all the various payments and receipts. Keep the old cash flow forecasts and compare them with the actual figures as they occur – this will help you improve the accuracy of your cash flow forecasting.

Some of your management bonus should be tied to the achievement of cash KPIs. Your financial controller could be targeted with reducing DSO, for example, while the sales manager could have customer cash receipts. There are many ways of achieving a cash-based bonus and the ones you choose will depend on the company's specific situation. The most important thing is to convey the importance of cash to the company – the cultural change of putting cash at the heart of the way a company thinks, plans and behaves has to come from the top.

Think beyond financial processes

The basic financial processes can be reviewed and improved in most companies, starting with credit control – making sure customer invoices are paid on time. An effective credit control function asks customers that do not pay on time why they don't, and is not afraid to reduce credit limits or to refuse to ship until old invoices are paid. Having a good dialogue between sales and receivables credit control, including the claw-back of sales commissions when customers do not pay within agreed timescales, is important too. A good credit control function or person will nearly always pay for itself many times over.

You can and should also review standard terms of payment, making the most use of e-payments, direct debits and other banking products to get payment more quickly. Exceptions to these standard terms should not be within the gift of the sales department but require approval from finance or even the CEO.

Invoices that are incorrect, for example by not referencing the customer's PO number or addressed to another company within the same group (e.g. ABC Group is likely to be a different company from ABC Interactive or ABC Innovations), give customers an excuse to delay payment. So get invoices right first time, as well as sent out on the day they are due to be sent.

Inventory management often focuses on the best-selling products, but these are typically the ones with the smallest inventory. Focus on the slow-selling products and those that represent the highest value in inventory. Can any be sold, or purchases reduced? This is in addition to having a good inventory control and planning system to make sure products can be shipped as quickly as possible with the smallest possible inventory levels.

Internal payments can also be delayed, as well as those to external suppliers. Can bonuses be moved from monthly to quarterly or from quarterly to annually? Sales commissions should be timed to be paid after the customer has paid the company and paid in arrears, for example quarterly. There are other ideas to be found, depending on your circumstances.

All of these are worthy, sensible and recommendations. Let's now consider some deeper structural changes, to make a dramatic difference to cash. To do so, we must start with the customer.

How good is your customer?

Think of a sale as a gift until it has been paid. So how likely is it that your customer will pay the bill at all or on time? Would you make that person or company such a gift? Of course not!

If you have the customer's balance sheet and P&L you can see whether they are a quick or slow payer and these accounts are easily available for all listed companies. Alternatively you can ask the customer for a recent set of accounts – this is not an uncommon request. It may require a few assumptions, but it is generally possible to estimate how promptly they pay or at least arm you with enough data to ask the right questions. Here's how:

1. Take the company's purchases for raw materials from the P&L (in other words, COGS less any personnel costs which form part of the COGS).
2. Divide that number into the trade payables figure from the balance sheet (if significant, you will need to exclude payables in connection with capital additions).

If you are supplying capital equipment to the company, you can do a similar calculation:

1. Take the company's capital additions from the balance sheet.
2. Divide that number into the trade payables figure from the balance sheet. (If significant, you will need to exclude payables in connection with COGS.)

Either way, if the number is low, the company pays quickly on average; if it is high, it pays slowly.

Let's take the example of two supermarket groups, Carrefour and Wal-Mart. Both operate in several countries, although Wal-Mart still has more stores in the USA than anywhere else, where the culture is to pay more promptly. Supermarkets have low margins, typically 20 to 25 per cent, so products purchased for resale dwarf all other costs and we will only consider those. From the annual reports of each company for 2009, these are the figures:

	Payables	COGS	Pay/COGS	Days
Wal-Mart	30,451	304,657	10%	36
Carrefour	16,800	68,098	25%	90

Which supermarket would you rather have as your customer? It certainly looks more attractive to sell to Wal-Mart. To be fair to Carrefour, it has its headquarters and many supermarkets in France, a country where payments are generally made more slowly than they are in the USA. So let's compare Carrefour with one of its French competitors, Auchan:

	Payables	COGS	Pay/COGS	Days
Auchan	7,131	30,294	24	86
Carrefour	16,800	68,098	25%	90

So it looks as if Carrefour behaves similarly to its peers. But from an NFO perspective, wouldn't you rather do business in the USA than in France, all other things being equal?

For a new customer, look at their balance sheet and P&L if it is available (ask the customer to provide them if they are not publicly available; it's a common request). Ask them to explain the difference if for example they claim to pay on 30 days but their balance sheet shows they pay on 90 days.

Product management

One of the biggest improvements can come from product management, which is perhaps not the most obvious place to look for cash.

The product management process helps determine what products to build, who they are sold to and through which channels. It covers the lifecycle of the product, from concept and market requirements through launch, sales ramp to product retirement. A pre-launch business case review ensures the product investment makes business sense in terms of expected sales and profits. Many departments are involved in these reviews, especially marketing and R&D. The review may be sophisticated enough to do a risk-adjusted return analysis, perhaps as a discounted cash flow.

What is probably missing from the review is the product's NFO requirement, as well as what steps can be taken to reduce or minimize NFO.

One of the best ways of reducing NFO within a product management process is to bring forward the date invoices are raised. This could include for example:

- A down-payment or a larger down-payment. If you are selling capital equipment for example, you should reasonably be able to ask for a percentage payment with order. If this is 20 per cent today, can it be increased to 30 per cent? If a down-payment is not possible for whatever reason, can there be two delivery options, one with a shorter delivery time and a down-payment, the other with no down-payment but longer delivery? This way the customer "reserves" his place in the queue.
- If invoices are raised on delivery to the customer, can this be moved back to the date of shipment? Or back from the date of shipment to the order point?
- How are support or extended warranty costs invoiced – can they be prepaid?
- If the product includes professional services, can a portion of the costs be invoiced in advance?
- Can the professional services be invoiced by milestone rather than waiting for project completion to raise the invoice?

And so on.

Here's a tip: if your product includes components or other items bought in from third parties, try and get at least the equivalent of the external cost covered by an up-front payment. Suppose you manufacture medical equipment that costs €10,000 to build and sells for €30,000. Your payment terms today are 100 per cent invoiced on shipment. Suppose you change the customer terms of payment to one third on receipt of order and two thirds on delivery, the payment to the supplier would be covered in time and amount by the customer payment.

Building NFO into the product management process should be as important a feature of the product as the product's technical prowess or marketing appeal.

To make sure the technical and marketing people take a serious look at NFO as they decide on the product introduction strategy, the required product profitability can be adjusted. For example, if the NFO is more than 10 per cent of sales, the required profitability could be increased. For an NFO that is negative, the required profitability could be set lower.

It is quite possible to have a product with a negative NFO: it's called a prepay product.

Designing a prepay product

We are used to paying in advance for many products already. Rent, insurance and package holidays are examples of products where we take it for granted that we will pay before receiving the product. Other items, such as utilities, we would never have expected to pay in advance, but this is increasingly the case.

Many companies could offer a prepay product but have not planned one or perhaps thought about it. Here are some examples:

- Few people thought a prepay telephone service was possible until the mobile phone industry introduced it in Italy. It was an instant hit with the less well-off because customers did not have to have a credit history to have a mobile phone. This has been mimicked by other utility companies with monthly "budget plans" and the like, which are all essentially prepaid products.
- Airlines and hotels used to take a credit card number to guarantee the reservation, but now they take the cash, presenting the offer as an "Internet special", for example. It's another form of prepayment.
- Microsoft and other software companies that license products like Windows built into other companies' products offer discounts for committed (i.e. prepaid) licenses. Typically an annual commitment to a volume of licenses is agreed and paid in advance. Alternatively, the customer can pay in arrears, but at a higher unit price.
- Maintenance and support is commonly invoiced annually in advance.
- Pretty much anything can be made into a prepay product; you just need to be creative!

Prepay products are not the same as improving payment terms – that's called credit control and everyone should do that – but rather designed as new products, with a different value proposition and perhaps even a different sales channel. You will need to give the customer something in exchange such as ease of use, reduced commitment and no credit control (as in the case of the prepay mobile phone), volume pricing or just lower pricing.

Using your suppliers as a source of funding

Using suppliers to reduce NFO is not about imposing worse terms on your suppliers in the way that large companies sometimes bully their suppliers. As a small company, you probably don't have the financial and market clout to demand better terms from suppliers. But consider what the supplier sees in you, or could see in you, as a customer. You're innovative, so being associated with you will probably help his reputation. You are small, but growing, and who knows how big your company will be? Companies are always interested in customers that grow. Also, the biggest concern for almost every supplier is customer loss – it is much more expensive to find a new customer than to hold on to an old one.

This can help with NFO: talk to the supplier and build a relationship with him. Tell him about your expansion plans and how you can grow together. Try and give him something he values, such as long-term requirement forecasts, or appointing him as the preferred supplier (whatever that may mean), or putting his logo on your product. Duracell for example, the battery manufacturer, has offered companies that produce products with disposable batteries better terms if "Powered by Duracell" or similar was printed in the user manual. Is there something similar that applies to your product? Once you have given the supplier something, explain that in exchange you want better terms of payment.

An extreme example of this is to integrate the supplier into the way you do business, with the supplier holding the inventory, supplying it as and when needed by you. Why would they do that? Because they have your business and that might be as important to them as the NFO is to you.

Reducing NFO is a powerful strategic tool, especially for a cash-strapped, high-growth company.

When cash gets really tight

Many start-ups face a cash crisis at some point in their development. Sometimes it is brought about by a delay in the next round of funding, other times by a delay in the take-off in sales. Or, as in the case of MissInge, it happens because sales are rising faster than planned.

Whatever the reason, there are some steps that can be taken to preserve the remaining cash and help the company back to stability.

First, get all the cash in one place, with one person in charge of the cheque book and other payment instruments. Develop a cash flow model that includes payments to suppliers so that you can tell them when they can expect payment. Review the model regularly, perhaps even every day.

The next step is to get paid more quickly by customers.

Use of direct debits and similar automatic payments

Most countries have an automatic way for suppliers to take money, with permission, directly from customers' bank accounts. It is presented as being easier than a manual payment but the main advantage for the supplier is that it reduces the risk that payments will be late or not made. Banks are also more likely to lend against direct debit payments than against the receivables book as a whole.

Direct debits work particularly well where the company has a large number of domestic customers that buy regularly, but otherwise you will need to look for other methods.

Early settlement discounts

The use of Early Settlement Discounts (ESD), where the supplier offers a discount in exchange for earlier payment by the customer, varies from country to country. In the USA for example, it is quite common; elsewhere it is unheard of. But that should not mean it is not worth trying, at least for an overseas transaction where cultural gaffes would more likely be excused.

A typical ESD works by offering a customer a choice between paying the full value of the invoice on normal terms (for example 45 days), and paying 98 per cent of the value of the invoice (i.e. taking a discount of 2 per cent) if payment is made within 15 days. This is equivalent to a 2 per cent discount for paying one month early, which for a company with spare cash can be very interesting, being a much greater return than they could get from having their spare cash in the bank.

An additional advantage of ESD is that in many countries the financial discount is not considered as a reduction in revenue but as a financial cost, so EBITDA is not affected. So the valuation of the company, which typically will be a multiple of EBITDA (valuations are covered elsewhere), should not be negatively affected by the use of ESD.

The theory behind ESD is simple: small companies have higher costs of capital because they are riskier than large companies. In theory, a perfect ESD is where the discount is set higher than the cost of capital for the customer but lower than the cost of capital of the supplier. In reality there needs to be quite a strong incentive for customers to make use of ESD, such as the eye-catching 2 per cent monthly return of the above example.

It's very easy to set up ESD. Just add to all invoices the following text: *"We operate an Early Settlement Incentive. If payment is received by us on or before 10 days from the date of this invoice, the amount paid can be reduced by 2 per cent"*. Also, don't forget to tell the sales department, because they can use it as a great argument when the customer complains about prices being too high! They are also the best way of getting the system known, understood and used. You should pay sales commissions and other bonuses on the full value of the invoice, not the discounted amount.

Triage your customers

Few companies prioritize their customers on the basis of how quickly they pay. But if your customer A pays a month quicker than your customer B, A should get priority in terms of service, product allocation and so on. It is hard to go back and get better payment terms from customer B once the relationship has been established and running for some time, but there are ways of bringing them into line.

Like product segmentation in marketing or the famous BCG matrix in business strategy, you can use a grid to segment your customers by NFO.

First, list the total sales by customer (you probably have that table already), then by profit (you may well not have that table to hand) and by average days taken to pay invoices (you almost certainly won't have that one!).

Divide the profit by the sales to give an average profit per sale. Rank order the customers by profit and, separately, by days taken to pay and place them into a matrix:

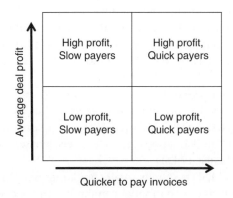

You can now make some decisions about how to treat your customers depending on how valuable they are to you in terms of profit and cash. What you do depends on your business, but how about the following?

- For the bottom-left quartile, where little profit is made from bad payers, increase the prices. Some customers will be lost, but does it matter? You could soften the blow by giving them a discount for moving to direct debit payments or early settlement discounts. This would move them to the bottom-left quartile, where little profit is made from good payers.
- What do you do with customers who pay well but where profits are too low? Is the business important in terms of keeping competitors at bay or to keep market share up? A good way is to encourage them to buy more, more profitable products, perhaps by introducing a premium product with more features and better support.
- For the top-left quartile, classic NFO reduction techniques can be used, such as offering Early Settlement Discounts and other incentives for paying early.
- You are now left with the top-right quartile, your very best customers. The worst thing to do it is to take them for granted, however good and long-term

the relationship is. Solidify the relationship however you can. Give them priority access to products, a strong say in the product roadmap and priority in support. And keep a close eye on their on-going satisfaction with your products and services.

What are the points in common in the various groups? Is it for example the sales channel, or the country, or the product? Understanding the root cause of the slow payment or low profitability will make it easier to solve.

For companies selling internationally, the country of the customer may make the difference. Companies in northern Europe tend to pay more quickly than those in southern Europe, for example. If that is the case, in a time of cash shortage, you may want to refocus your sales efforts accordingly.

Triage your products

Similarly, products can be sorted by profitability and by NFO. Sort the products by total gross margin (as with the customers, you can repeat by percentage gross margin to see whether that produces anything significantly different).

Calculate the NFO by product by looking at the purchases, inventory and how quickly customers pay, as shown previously. Then sort the products into this grid:

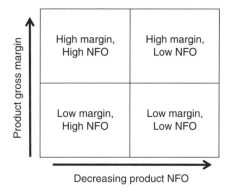

As with the customers, the most attractive products are in the top-right quadrant. The others may be able to migrate there, by being treated in different ways:

- Products in the left quartiles, with high NFO, should be put through a product management review to work out how the NFO could be reduced. Can suppliers be paid later? Can product inventory levels be reduced? Would customers agree to pay some or all in advance?

- Products in the bottom quartiles are of below average profitability – why is this and can anything be done to improve profitability?
- The bottom-left quartile is the least attractive, because they require lots of NFO and generate little profit. If the situation cannot be improved, consider discontinuing the product.
- The bottom-right quartile contains products that require little cash but generate little profit. If prices cannot be increased, consider putting no further development or marketing effort into them; just allow them to tick along.
- The top-left products are interesting because they are profitable, but they absorb lots of cash which the company probably does not have. Look at NFO reduction techniques such as ESD, phased payments and inventory reduction.
- The company's focus should be on the products in the top-right quartile which require the least cash to produce the most profit. Focus the company's marketing effort on these products. Give the sales team more commission for sales of this class of product. Run volume promotions.

If the company is really short of cash, the best thing to do is to focus on products and customers that tie up the least amount of cash.

Episode 6

Back at the Bank

In business, you sometimes have to kill your favourite children.

John Harvey-Jones

It is a few minutes before her next meeting with Hans, and Grace is a little nervous. Although she had worked hard since the last meeting with the bank, she still needs their support to be able to continue trading. Sometimes Hans is hard to read and if he really refused to grant the agreed credit line, she would probably have to wind MissInge up, or enter a fire sale.

The bank too has been active, with an auditor poring all over the financial projections as Grace and her team grappled with suppliers and customers in the race to reduce NFO.

"Good morning, Grace", Hans welcomes her warmly. Was that a hint of a smile? thinks Grace.

"Good morning, Hans."

"Let's get straight into the meeting, shall we? How did you get on, Grace?" asks Hans.

"We divided into two teams, one looking at inventory and manufacturing NFO and the other examining ways of being paid more quickly by customers. I will start with the manufacturing side, which I led," says Grace. "Joe led the other team on reducing accounts receivable NFO."

"Obviously our focus was on the microfibre, because that was such a large element of the NFO and it was frankly mad to have the supplier ship it here rather than to China."

"We have reached an agreement with the supplier that covers marketing as well as credit. They were understandably not enthusiastic about just giving a large amount of credit to a small company with a history of losses, but once their marketing team became involved, it became easier for them to see the attraction of dealing with us," continues Grace.

63

"What's the agreement with them?" asks Hans.

"They now supply the microfibre directly to our local company *MissInge in China*, with 60 days' payment terms. The parent company provides a guarantee, but otherwise all the financial transactions take place in China."

"MissInge in China is a woofy, isn't it?" interrupts Hans.

"Wholly owned foreign enterprise, yes," confirms Grace. "We own it."

"The price for the microfibre is the same as we pay at the moment; in fact it will go down in time with the volumes we are forecasting. They are providing us enough credit for our predicted volumes for the next 12 months, at which time we will review the arrangement," says Grace.

"What do they get in return?" asks Hans.

"Me," replies Grace, a little sheepishly. "I will appear in a set of advertisements endorsing their product. They also get to attach a small promotional leaflet to each jacket. It's not that bad a deal – we got what we wanted."

"What's the effect on NFO?" asks Hans, ever-focused on the numbers.

"I'll come to that," Grace replies. "I just want to cover, if I may, some other things that make quite a difference."

"We have a term sheet in place with one of the big logistics companies for them to take over the whole supply chain. They will collect from the factory in China, ship the products to Europe, hold any inventory and deliver to the customers. Included in the deal is our warehouse, which they are buying, together with some of our staff."

"The costs work out about the same, but the big advantage comes in China, where we are no longer limited to shipping once a month in order to get to reasonable shipping costs. As they are consolidating the shipment of our products with those of other companies manufacturing in China, they can ship small quantities for the same price. They have ships leaving constantly."

"We have also agreed with the suppliers of the other components to receive shipments every week rather than every month, which reduces inventory in the factory."

"Overall we can halve the current 45-day manufacturing and inventory cycle by switching from monthly to weekly shipments," Grace continues, "and halve the inventory in the warehouse here, an overall saving of 30 days."

"I thought you were really attached to the warehouse – your name on the door, that sort of thing," commented Hans.

"I can't tell you how painful it was, it was just ghastly. I have worked with Mary on and off for much of my career and I felt I was betraying her by selling her off like a commodity to a faceless global logistics organization," says Grace, with some evident pain. "She put a brave face on it but I could tell that underneath she was really upset. But without the logistics deal we would not have been where we need to be in terms of NFO."

"So where does that get the NFO?" asks Hans, not wanting to dwell on the emotional side of what Grace had had to do.

"I thought you would want to come back to the numbers, Hans!" says Grace, smiling. "Do you remember the PowerPoint slide you showed in the last meeting with the total manufacturing and payment days? I've got it here – let's look at it again because the comparison is quite striking."

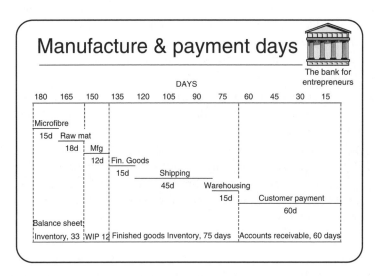

"We've attacked each of the items, with the following result," says Grace. "I've left it on the bank's template to make it easy to compare, but the slide is a little busy."

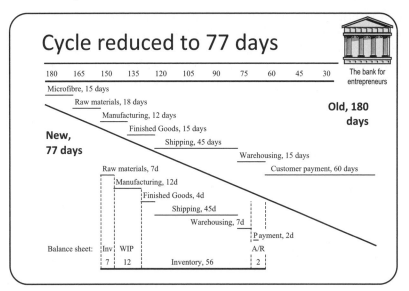

"As I mentioned, the microfibre just becomes a normal component in the manufacturing cycle and no longer needs to be paid for in advance. The move from a monthly to a weekly cycle saves 22 days in manufacturing, and shipping and inventory in the European warehouse is reduced to seven days.

"The manufacturing and inventory portion has been reduced from 120 days to 75. I hadn't thought about this until we started working on it detail, but there is an added business benefit: we can make changes to the products we are selling and marketing more quickly," explains Grace. "We can respond to changing market needs with new designs, colours and styles. We are able to have the hottest-selling products in stock at the times they are wanted."

"So you've cut manufacturing and inventory time by nearly a half. Well done!" congratulates Hans. "And the accounts receivable look pretty impressive too."

"We did better, if anything!" says Grace, smiling. "Joe managed this section, although we discussed it regularly together. I never expected a salesman to get into the financial nitty-gritty but he loved it! He's not able to be here today, but I know enough to present it to you in some detail. If there are any questions I can't answer, I can follow those up afterwards."

"OK."

"We started by sorting the customers by how fast they pay, and realized pretty quickly how different they all are. The average payment might be 60 days, but it is not the case that everyone pays in 60 days. We do for example about 10 per cent of our business through the website and on eBay, where we get instant payment."

"We identified four basic customer types. First there are the large chains that have department stores all over the country. They don't pay very quickly, but they do sell a lot. They are our largest customer group, with 35 per cent of our sales and they only pay in 73 days on average. Officially most of them have 60-day payment terms with us, but we can wait up to three months to be paid."

"Next there is the small retailer. There are quite a few of those, normally owner-run. Some of them we don't provide credit to and most of them pay pretty promptly in 30 days. Some are a little slower but they know they won't get any more stock until they pay for the previous shipment. They are important because they are 30 per cent of our business and they help us become better known in just about every high street. Payment is made by this group on average in 30 days."

"The third group can best be called the international importers. In some countries, such as Russia and Japan, we use an importer who buys stock and sells to all the shops and customers in their country. It is easier for us to get into a country that we don't know this way, or where we don't have good contacts. It turns out they are terrible payers, normally paying on 90 days. They are about 25 per cent of our business."

"Finally there is the website and eBay, which as I mentioned is about 10 per cent. This is a rather neglected area because the large chains in particular are not keen for us to sell directly, as this competes with them. So we've mostly sold to our club members," explains Grace.

"Club members?" asks Hans.

"We run a sort of fan club for our most committed customers. They can get early access to new designs, get invited to our fashion shows, receive a newsletter – that sort of thing."

"We have not really exploited the web as a direct channel because we didn't want to upset our resellers," explains Grace.

"I see," says Hans. "So how have you managed to improve things?"

"We started with the worst offenders, the importers. They pay badly because they want to match payments they make with cash from their customers. So they wait until they are paid before paying us. We might get upset with them but there is little we can do to make sure they pay."

"Are they perhaps unable to pay quicker? Are they really small companies?"

"No. In fact many of them are big companies and are quite capable of providing some funding," answers Grace.

"It was clear that we might have to withdraw completely from some countries if we could not resolve our financial problems. So we decided to be aggressive. We announced that all international importers would have to buy directly from China, which we could arrange through our new logistics partner. And they could either pay with a letter of credit or up-front. Either way it means we get the money before the goods leave China, because our local bank in China advances the cash against a letter of credit."

"To soften the blow, we improved the margins to offset the financing cost for them," explains Grace.

"How did that go down?" asks Hans.

"Well, this is all quite new so we are still dealing with the backlash and I am sure we will lose some business. I estimate with sales to this group falling from 25 per cent to about 20 per cent of total sales. But overall the idea has been accepted not least because they feel they will get quicker deliveries by buying directly from China, and they do like the extra margin which enables them to compete against grey imports. It's not that straightforward because our ERP system in China does not yet handle invoicing and payments but that will get sorted out."

"The amazing thing about this is that we will have gone from being paid 60 days in arrears to being paid 52 days in advance," she adds.

"Fifty-two days, how come?" asks Hans.

"Forty-five days for the shipping time from China and seven days for the average time the products are held in inventory in our warehouse," explains Grace.

"I see."

"Next, we decided to change strategy and sell more products directly to customers. Our e-commerce site is being revamped and we will run promotions, email campaigns and so on to encourage customers to buy directly from us. We believe we can get to 25 per cent of sales via the Internet fairly quickly."

"That is going to reduce the sales going though the shops from 30 per cent to about 25 per cent, and to the chains from 35 per cent to about 30 per cent. We have spoken to all the key chains and to the independent shops that we know best, and there is grudging acceptance. Everyone sells directly over the web these days, so we are hardly a pioneer in that sense," Grace explains, pausing for a moment to help herself to a bottle of water.

"That sounds pretty comprehensive. You've achieved a lot in a very short time. Is there anything else?" asks Hans.

"Just one other thing – we looked to see who might be willing and able to pay early and, after making some enquiries, we have offered the chains an early settlement discount. More than half have indicated they will take it up and I expect average payments for that group to drop to 30 days."

"We take a margin hit on that early settlement discount and on the improved margins to the importers but that is more than offset by the increased direct sales via the website," continues Grace.

"Can you summarize the overall NFO effect for me?" asks Hans.

"Of course, the headline figure is we expect to reduce accounts receivable NFO from 60 days to two days," says Grace, smiling.

"TWO days? That's astonishing. Can you show me on the whiteboard, please?" says Hans.

"Here goes," says Grace, walking up to the whiteboard. "First, this is where we were."

	Sales in %	Days
Chains	35	73
International	30	90
Independent	25	30
Website, eBay	10	0
Average payment		60

After a short pause, she steps forward again and as if to emphasize how much things are changing at MissInge, she adds the words "Then" and "Now" at the top followed by the new numbers.

"And this is what I think we will achieve: an average payment of just two days."

	THEN		NOW	
	Sales in %	Days	Sales in %	Days
Chains	35	73	30	30
International	30	90	25	−52
Independent	25	30	20	30
Website, eBay	10	0	25	0
Average payment		60		2

"What's the overall effect on NFO?" asks Hans.

"It drops to just under 10 per cent," answers Grace.

"Can we see the effect on the balance sheet, please?" asks Hans.

"OK. Again, we have used your template."

Simplified Balance Sheet - new

The bank for entrepreneurs

Balance (000€)	2007	2008	2009	2010	2011	2012	2013
NFO	59	481	853	984	1,447	1,758	2,109
Fixed assets	20	135	2,071	3,853	3,830	3,459	3,272
Net assets - to be financed	79	616	2,924	4,838	5,276	5,216	5,381
Long Term Debt	500	1,000	1,075	1,156	1,242	1,335	1,436
Equity	0	1,543	3,254	2,766	3,140	4,239	5,961
Liabilities & equity - financing	500	2,543	4,329	3,922	4,382	5,574	7,397
Cash surplus (+), Credit (-)	421	1,927	1,405	-916	-894	358	2,016
Cash generated per year	421	1,506	-523	-2,320	22	1,252	1,658

"Unless I'm mistaken, there is no change to the asset line. Why is that, with the sale of the warehouse to the logistics company?" asks Hans.

"They operate our assets; we continue to own them. Unfortunately they declined to write us a cheque," explained Grace with a wry smile. "Similarly, the profit is not affected by all these changes, just the cash. As you can see from this next slide, we now need about a million euros rather than five, and from 2012 we expect to have positive cash again."

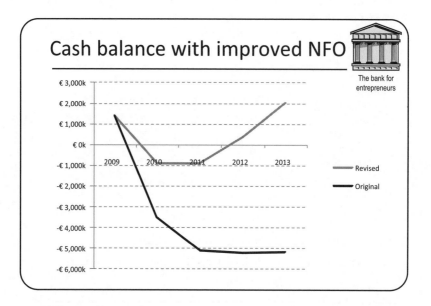

"If I remember correctly," Hans says, "you are expecting profits to rise from about 3 per cent to about 8 per cent. So with an NFO of about 10 per cent, the sustainable growth rate is still less than the 75 per cent of the high scenario we discussed last time. Did you forecast the cash position if you grow more quickly?"

"Yes, we modelled different growth rates now that I understand the sensitivity of growth and cash. Here is the graph of the cash with the two growth rates of 75 per cent and those in the current business plan," explains Grace.

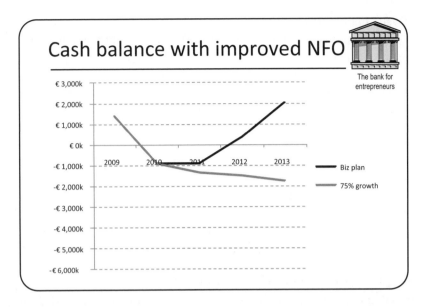

"Although it shows cash continuing to deteriorate, I think it's manageable. For example, we have only modelled the personnel costs. There are probably savings to be had there, which would enable us to keep our heads above water cash-wise. And to be honest it would be a great problem to have!"

"I'm very impressed, Grace," says Hans. "Very impressed. You and the team have really taken this issue to heart and have done an outstanding job. I think what you are saying is there is no change to the P&L at all – sales and margins stay the same more or less – just the balance sheet is affected?"

"That's right. The reduction in margin from the ESD and better terms to the international importers is offset by the increase in higher margin sales from our website and via eBay."

"Let's talk about the facility for a few moments," suggests Hans. "The package at the last round of equity fundraising had the investors providing €4 million in equity funding, provided in two equal tranches. The second tranche is conditional on us providing a credit line of €500,000, although this is a buffer – the model did not show your actually needing the money."

"That's right. We wanted to have a buffer to help with erratic payments, unexpected marketing costs, that sort of thing," says Grace.

"Clearly what has changed is that the company needs about a million more than we all expected at the time of the last round. Have you thought about that? Are you looking for us to extend our facility to provide some kind of structural finance?" asks Hans.

"Well I hope you are now more comfortable with the company and that the facility is put in place. If you can provide us with an additional million, that would be great."

"The bank would not increase the facility to cover the extra requirements – that's too much for us. We do have a venture debt arm, which offers typically three-year term loans. I would think you might either approach them or ask your existing investors for another million. To be clear," emphasizes Hans, "we will only extend the facility if the company has at least an additional million in equity or long-term debt which would be subordinated to our facility."

"I am ahead of you for once, Hans," says Grace, smiling. "I have already approached the investors and they are prepared to make an investment of a further €1 to €2 million; in fact we already have the term sheet. The valuation will not be the last round's but at the one before. That should not make a big difference because we raising so little. And otherwise the terms will be the same. With a bit of luck," she adds, smiling.

"In that case, we have a solution, Grace. I will write to you to confirm the bank will extend the facility once the new equity is in place," confirms Hans.

Just as she is about to thank Hans, Grace's iPhone rings.

"That thing always goes off at the worst possible time. I must remember to switch it to silent!" Grace looks at the screen, then turns to Hans.

"It's Daniel, my angel investor who helped the company get started. Hopefully this is good news, so please excuse me, Hans. I would like to take the call, if you don't mind."

"Go ahead, not a problem."

"Grace, this is Dan."

"Hi Dan. I've just finished here with Hans. It looks like we're back on track."

"Grace, that's not the reason I called, although I'm of course pleased it went well. I'm really sorry, Grace, but I'm phoning to let you know I cannot accept the proposed additional investment of €1 to €2 million by the investors."

"Why on earth not? Without it the bank won't provide the facility, we don't get the €2 million from the last round and then where will we be?"

"Grace, you know how keen I am to see you and MissInge succeed, but what you're asking me to do is to throw away my investment."

"How can that be, Dan? I think the company can end up being worth a lot. We can sell to one of the big fashion groups or even perhaps IPO. Can't we?" Grace asks a little anxiously.

"I've had the opportunity to understand MissInge's capital structure a lot better over the past few days. As you know, I have made a number of investments in start-up companies so I am quite familiar with the way VCs invest. I also went through the new term sheet. If we take in this new money, I believe there is no scenario where the ordinary shares will ever be worth anything."

"But you own 15 per cent or so now, don't you? Even at the low valuation, you'll still have 10 per cent I would have thought. And we should be able to sell the business for €20 million in the next two to three years – that's €2 million to you, isn't it?"

"Yes, I will have perhaps about 10 per cent of the shares, but not 10 per cent of the economic value of the company. If you sell the company for €20 million, I would barely get my original investment back. I'm sorry, Grace, but I feel either I've been misled or you don't understand your cap table. Both are problems as far as I'm concerned. I'm sorry to be so harsh but I'm from the old school where it is more important in business to make money for your shareholders than to make award-winning products."

Chapter 6
Share Structures and Shareholders

All animals are equal, but some animals are more equal than others.

George Orwell

Entrepreneurs, in their impatience and excitement of raising money from investors, often give away much more of their company than they think they're giving – and it's generally avoidable. It's not because the VC wouldn't cut a fairer deal; it's because the entrepreneur doesn't even bother to ask or negotiate on key terms. They're too busy fighting tooth and nail over the wrong things.

The unwritten relationship between the entrepreneur and the Venture Capitalist is a simple one: the entrepreneur brings his ideas, experience and sweat while the VC provides the money. They then share in the wealth created.

If no wealth is created, there should be nothing to share. For example, if a VC invests €1 million for 50 per cent of a company, and the company is then sold for only €1 million, it seems only fair the VC should get their money back and the entrepreneur should get nothing. Getting their money back first is called a Liquidation Preference and is one of the reasons why a VC's shares are worth more than the simple percentage arithmetic might imply.

Venture Capital firms are fund managers, meaning the majority of the money to be invested comes from others, called Limited Partners or LPs. The LPs might be institutions such as pension funds and insurance companies looking to diversify their investments. The money raised is normally held in a fund and invested for a period of seven to ten years before being distributed back to LPs. VC managers are called General Partners, or GPs, and often invest their own money, perhaps 1% to 5% of the fund.

The VC business model is to build a portfolio of investments, some of which will be successful, some not. VCs aim for the portfolio of investments in a fund as a whole to make a profit, accepting that a fund will lose money on some investments and make money on others. VC firms make money by charging LPs a management fee as a percentage of the fund and by taking a share of the profits once fund returns exceed a certain agreed threshold, called the hurdle rate. Typical fees are an annual charge of 2 per cent of the fund plus a bonus of 20 per cent of the net gains once it exceeds an agreed target of about 8 to 10 per cent per year net of the management fees (the hurdle rate), over the fund life of seven to ten years.

A small VC with, for example, a €20 million fund would then receive €400,000 a year in management fees, which would only support the costs of a very small office. The VC would start to receive the bonus once the fund value exceeds the original €20 million compounded at the hurdle rate per year for the life of the fund. For a hurdle rate of 10 per cent and a fund life of seven years, for example, compound interest would make the original €20 million worth about €40 million at the end of the life of the fund.

Let's suppose the fund does well and becomes worth €50 million at the end of the seven-year period. The partners of the VC firm would then earn a bonus of €2 million (20 per cent of the return in excess of 10 per cent per year). This bonus from the excess performance of the fund is called "carried interest" or "carry" for short.

Over the seven-year period, the VC firm's income in this example would be €2.8 million from management fees and €2 million from the carry. The management fees may well be lower, being sometimes based on committed capital (the fund size) and sometimes on invested capital.

So it is important for a VC to have good returns on funds, because that increases the carry, and for the funds to be large, because that increases the management fee. Some VCs' funds are so large that they become more interested in the management fee than the carry, but generally a VC will aim for the management fee to cover daily expenses and for his wealth to be created by the carry.

VCs need to make money on all or nearly all funds, because that will determine how easily the VC can raise the next fund as well how much can be earned from the carry. Carry is generally not negative (meaning the VC does not pay the LP if the fund performance is less than the hurdle). Instead, if fund performance is poor, the VC may struggle to attract enough investment into the new fund, so the size of the fund is not as large as they would like in order to earn enough management fees. Perhaps the VC can't raise a new fund at all, in which case the VC will eventually go out of business.

This creates two problems when brought together with the world of entrepreneurs. First, the individual entrepreneur is only making one bet at a time so his outcome is binary: he will only make money if his venture is successful. There is no portfolio to smooth out the return.

Secondly, the largest constituent of a VC's portfolio is often the so-called "living dead", the unflattering term for companies that are operating but are unlikely to create great shareholder value. Perhaps sales are not growing as expected, or the technology has not caught the market's imagination. Recognizing the need to show returns on all funds, the VC's attention has shifted to making a return from these firms, the living dead, leaving little or nothing for the entrepreneur.

In other words, the emphasis has shifted from the original deal of sharing in the upside to protecting the downside on the non-performing companies.

Sparks can fly when the entrepreneur sees the VC keep all the proceeds from the sale of the entrepreneur's business, especially when an entrepreneur has created real value. But it is then too late; the structure needs to be got right at the time of investment, ideally at the time of the first VC investment, as future rounds will often mirror the first structure.

VCs may also drip-feed investment into companies. An initial tranche is invested, with the remainder being available to draw down later, perhaps attached to milestones or subject to a "material adverse change" clause. The justification is that the LP too only invests in the VC's fund as and when funds are needed (the expression used is that the funds are "called" when needed).

So the company can only have the money if it is performing according to its business plan, in effect meaning the investment is conditional on the company doing as well or better than planned.

Entrepreneurs naturally focus on the valuation a VC places on the company when the investment is made and what percentage of the company a VC holds, whereas the VC will trade those off against ways of making the VC fund's shareholding more valuable under different scenarios. In fact in many ways the VC does not care too much about the valuation, in that there are more important issues to agree on. Nor should the entrepreneur care so much about the valuation.

Pushed to an extreme, the shareholder numbers quoted by an entrepreneur can be completely meaningless. An assertion such as "We raised €5 million at a valuation of €20 million, leaving the founders with 75 per cent of the company" is almost certainly all wrong. It might instead be "We raised €1 million with a possibility of up to €4 million more. Fully invested, the founders will have between 0 per cent and close to 75 per cent of the company, depending on when the company is sold and for how much."

The good news is that if you understand the way a VC values a company and structures an investment, you can optimize your return. To be as precise in this as possible, we asked 421 VC firms in Europe for their input on what common practice is and what aspects of an investment are negotiable. We have included the results against each relevant term in the term sheet (the letter that precedes the full-blown investment agreement). The full results of the survey can be found in Appendix 2.

So here's how to win:

Liquidation preferences

As mentioned earlier, a liquidation preference gives the VC his or her money back ahead of the entrepreneur and, on the face of it at least, is a fair term.

Let's consider a company that is owned 50 per cent by the entrepreneur and 50 per cent by the VC. If the company is sold for the amount the VC has invested, the VC will receive everything. If the company is sold for twice the investment (or more), the VC and entrepreneur share the proceeds equally. The relative proceeds can be graphed like this:

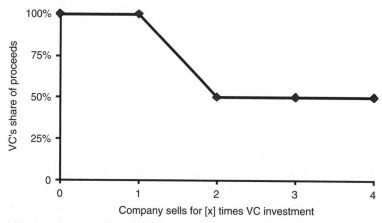

Multiple liquidation preferences

Sometimes the VC will ask for a multiple liquidation preference. A 2x liquidation preference means the VC first gets twice his investment back before any of the proceeds go to the entrepreneur. This is most likely to happen when the VC feels he is in a strong negotiation position.

This is the graph for a 2x liquidation preference, using the same example of a company owned half by the VC and half by the entrepreneur. The VC gets the first €2 million of the sales value of the company and the entrepreneur receives the next €2 million, after which they share the proceeds. This means the VC will get more than the supposedly 50 per cent entrepreneur shareholder unless and until the company is worth four times what the VC invested.

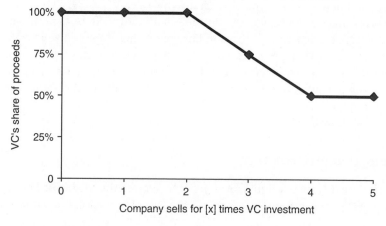

Liquidation preferences are very common in term sheets, with 78 per cent of VCs using them as a matter of course. A further 20 per cent use them sometimes. As they are misunderstood, or perhaps because of misplaced entrepreneur hubris, they are fiercely negotiated only 63 per cent of the time, 30 per cent sometimes and 7 per cent just nod it through. That's a mistake, as they are surprisingly negotiable, at least in the way they work – it is harder to negotiate away their presence.

The VCs were asked in some detail about their opening gambit on multiple liquidation preferences and where the negotiations end up, the results of which are summarized in this graph:

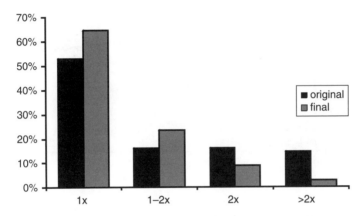

Many first term sheets have liquidation preferences in excess of 1x, but most are reduced to close to 1x after negotiation. If the role of liquidation preferences is to protect the VC's capital rather than to provide accelerated returns, then anything above 1x is hard to defend. Before negotiation a third of liquidation preferences are over 2x, but this drops to little more than 10 per cent once negotiations are concluded.

The good news is that after negotiations liquidation preferences mostly end up in the right place, being 1x the VC investment.

Liquidation preferences are hard to remove later, but a sensible place to end up is 1x. Anything more needs some explanation from the investor. In any event, assuming the company ends up delivering a positive return, liquidation preferences don't matter, except when they are so-called participating liquidation preferences.

Participating liquidation preferences

Without "participation", the entrepreneur receives all the proceeds from the sale of the business once the liquidation preference has been paid, until the amount each has received is back in proportion to their ownership.

With "participation", the VC "participates" in the proceeds, meaning that he receives his share of the proceeds in addition to the liquidation preference immediately. In our example, once the liquidation preference has been paid, the entrepreneur and the VC each get 50 per cent of the additional proceeds.

This is also called "double-dipping" because the VC essentially receives his portion of the proceeds twice. This is the graph of how the proceeds are shared, using the same example.

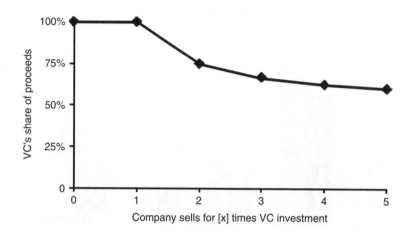

Note that with this mechanism the entrepreneur's share of the proceeds never reaches 50 per cent, however much the company is sold for. So much for the entrepreneur's claim: "I own 50 per cent."

Of term sheets with liquidation preferences, 80 per cent include participation, but it is a relatively negotiable term. Only 7 per cent would not agree to discuss, and 42 per cent are unlikely to remove participation, but the remaining 31 per cent might remove participation. This is one term that is certainly worth fighting! For example, try including a term that removes participation once valuations exceed 2x the original VC investment, or at the next round of funding.

Entrepreneurs tend to think of one investment round in isolation, but it is a rare company that manages to survive with a single injection of cash. Multiple rounds with participating liquidation preferences can create a mountain to climb, so it is important at each round to see how liquidation preferences can be reduced or removed, or at least to have the participation removed.

Another consideration is whether and how these terms might apply in the event of an IPO. In a listed company all shareholders are equal and removing the liquidation preferences at the time of listing just involves issuing more shares to the VC. Would the investors perhaps agree to waive the liquidation preference at IPO?

Accrued dividends

In addition to the liquidation preference, the VC fund might ask for a special dividend which would only be paid on his shares, not on the entrepreneur's. Some VCs argue that without a regular income from his investment, the LP might prefer to leave his money in an interest-bearing account, and that a dividend should be the minimum return to the investor in the event of the shares not growing in value.

Instead of being paid in cash, which the company may well not have while it is growing and perhaps not making profits, the dividends accrue and are paid out as a lump sum when the company is sold, or additional shares are issued.

The dividends may or may not compound, but either way, time is of the essence in selling the business because it will become increasingly expensive to pay off the investor.

Dividend clauses are by no means universal in term sheets. Some 63 per cent of survey respondents always or sometimes seek dividends in term sheets, but only 33 per cent use them systemically. In fact, only 18 per cent of completed term sheets include an accrued dividend clause. Interestingly 53 per cent claim these clauses are rarely contentious during negotiation. So if your venture is likely to take some time to develop, grow and reach fruition, try to negotiate the removal of dividends or some combination of the removal of compounding or a reduced interest rate.

Pre-money valuation

This is the most hotly negotiated subject – how much the company is worth. In fact, the VC is often quite happy for it to be hotly contested, as it detracts attention from bigger issues.

His logic goes like this: first he looks at the exit value, how much the company could be worth when it is sold or listed on a stock market. Let's assume he thinks it could be worth €20 million. His firm will have a threshold of how much they want to make from each investment. If, for example, that is €10 million, the VC firm needs to own 50 per cent of the company. It matters less how much he pays for it, because more money will go in to the company in later rounds anyway, when he will look to maintain his percentage ownership.

The initial offer is to invest €1 million for 50 per cent of the company, a pre-money valuation (meaning before the money goes into the company) of €1 million and a post-money valuation (the moment after the investment goes into the company) of €2 million. The entrepreneur insists on a valuation of at least €2.5 million. Not a problem: the VC invests €1.25 million for the same 50 per cent and is relaxed in the knowledge that the company has a longer cash runway until the next round. At the same time, the VC demands concessions in terms of liquidation preferences, participation, accrued dividends and so on. The entrepreneur thinks he has negotiated a great deal in that his company is now worth €2.5 million. In fact, he would be better off taking a lower valuation, with a simpler and less onerous share structure.

Post-money valuation, using the above example of an investment of €1 million for 50 per cent of the company, is calculated as:

$$\text{post-money valuation} = \frac{\text{amount of investment}}{\text{investment ownership}} = \frac{\text{€1 million}}{50\%} = \text{€2 million}$$

The pre-money valuation is just the post-money valuation minus the amount of the investment. In this example it is €2 million – €1 million = €1 million.

As the investor shares have a different value from the common or ordinary shares that the founders have, the pre-money valuation calculation is arguably close to meaningless.

Of term sheets, 99 per cent include a pre-money valuation for the investment, with 94 per cent claiming it is a key topic of negotiation. The VCs have done well to create such a diversion away from other factors that are less well understood by entrepreneurs.

Anti-dilution

In its simplest form, the anti-dilution right grants the investors more shares if future investment rounds are at lower valuations than the current round.

When investors invest in an early stage company, it is often connected with a milestone, such as the commercially available product, or a sales milestone. Most small companies do not meet their product launch milestones and many do not see sales ramp up as quickly as they had first planned or hoped. It is easy for valuations to be driven down at a time when the company is desperate for cash, using delays in product delivery and commercial ramp as justification.

If the entrepreneur has traded a higher valuation for more onerous investment terms, he may find himself having lost both with the anti-dilution clause, ending up with a smaller shareholding and a bad investment agreement.

Anti-dilution can be calculated in different ways, for example will all rounds be affected, or just the most recent? Is it based on the current round price, or a weighted average between the previous and current rounds? Does it apply to all shareholders or only those that invest in the current round? The exact terms need careful studying, modelling and negotiation.

Anti-dilution terms enable the possibility of a significant shift in wealth from the entrepreneur to the VC, or rather the acceleration in the reduction of the entrepreneur's shareholding.

Take the example of a company that, after a round of investment, is today worth €10 million. The entrepreneur owns 800 shares and the VC 200 shares, an 80/20 per cent split. Each of the 1,000 shares is therefore worth €10,000 and the entrepreneur's holding is worth €8 million. The pre-money (i.e. pre-investment) valuation of the company is €10 million.

The company is in urgent need of a cash injection of €1 million which the entrepreneur assumes will be made at the same valuation as the previous round. That would mean the new investment would buy 100 shares and would increase the number of shares in circulation to 1,100. This is the effect:

	Shares		%	
	Before	After	Before	After
Entrepreneur	800	800	80	73
VC – old	200	200	20	18
VC – new		100		9
Total	1,000	1,100	100	100

The post-money valuation of the business is €11 million, which can either be calculated as the pre-money valuation plus the new investment (i.e. €10 million plus €1 million) or by looking at how much ownership the new investor got: 9.1 per cent. The post-money valuation is calculated as:

$$\text{post-money valuation} = \frac{\text{investment}}{\text{new shares}} = \frac{\text{€1 million}}{9.1\%} = \text{€11 million}$$

But the investor smells blood. Due to the urgent need for cash, the investor insists the new investment comes in at a pre-money valuation of €5 million. There has been no change in the company's prospects – it's just that the VC has the upper hand in the negotiations. Reluctantly, the entrepreneur agrees to the new valuation so the price per share drops to €5,000 and 200 new shares are bought. The new ownership looks like this:

	Shares		%	
	Before	After	Before	After
Entrepreneur	800	800	80	67
VC – old	200	200	20	17
VC – new		200		17
Total	1,000	1,200	100	100

The VC then invokes the anti-dilution clause, which issues the VC fund enough new shares at no cost to compensate for the lower pricing. As the price per share has halved, the original VC is issued with 200 new shares, doubling the original holding:

	Shares		%	
	Before	After	Before	After
Entrepreneur	800	800	80	57
VC – old	200	400	20	29
VC – new		200		14
Total	1,000	1,400	100	100

This round of investment looks very expensive, with the entrepreneur's shareholding falling from 80 per cent to 57 per cent. The VC's share has increased from 18 per cent to 43 per cent, or an extra 25 per cent of the share capital. The effective valuation is now just €4 million, a significant drop from the original €11 million:

$$\text{valuation after dilution} = \frac{\text{investment}}{\text{new shares}} = \frac{\text{€1 million}}{25\%} = \text{€4 million}$$

Anti-dilution can be a way of dealing with valuation gaps between the VC and the entrepreneur. The VC can agree to a high valuation with anti-dilution in the knowledge that he will most likely receive more shares later to bring his ownership to where, in his view, it should have been at the beginning.

Anti-dilution is a one-way process unfortunately, as there is no adjustment to the shareholdings if the valuation is much higher in a later round. Take the case of a company that starts out being owned half by the VC and half by the entrepreneur. There is a down-round, where the anti-dilution clause results in the value of the entrepreneur's holding being reduced. This graph is one way of looking at the effect:

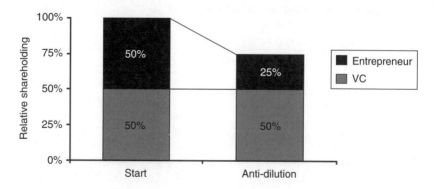

This is equivalent to the entrepreneur owning one-third and the VC two-thirds. If the company then has an investment round, even quite a modest one, the entrepreneur is quickly at the point where his shareholding is very small. Here it is on a graph:

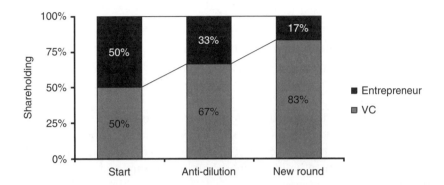

Down-rounds are quite common. Fenwick and West, a US law firm, publishes a quarterly survey of venture fundraising, including the direction of price changes for companies receiving funding compared with their previous round. In 2008 and 2009 the percentage of down rounds varied from 12 per cent to 46 per cent, meaning up to every other round was at a lower valuation.

To protect yourself against down-rounds, it is important to understand the detail of how anti-dilution terms might be used and to work to limit their effect through time or other restrictions in the investment agreement.

It is hard to avoid some form of anti-dilution clause, as 95 per cent of term sheets include the provision. Interestingly, it is a hot negotiation topic in only 39 per cent of cases. VCs also regularly agree to soften the terms of the anti-dilution to a weighted average price or to certain rounds.

The takeaway is that while it is hard to avoid anti-dilution, it should be possible to agree more entrepreneur-friendly terms.

Other considerations terms when negotiating with VCs

There are a number of other commonly used terms in term sheets. Their importance and frequency of use can be found in Appendix 2. A good lawyer, with direct experience in VC investments, is essential to understand the terms in detail and to help you achieve a fair balance. Remember to read all the legal documents yourself carefully.

In terms of safeguarding entrepreneur wealth, or at least making sure that everyone understands the implications of the round of investment being contemplated, there is nothing better than to build a simple exit spreadsheet, to show who will receive what under various assumptions of exit prices and timings.

At the very least, the finalized term sheet should include a share capital table so that everyone can see who owns what once the investment is concluded.

This is the basic structure:

gross proceeds = sale price + surplus cash + cash from option exercise

net proceeds = gross proceeds − debt − transaction costs

proceeds to ordinary shareholders = net proceeds − liquidation
preferences − dividends

Net proceeds are distributed according to the rights of each share class, and may vary from round to round, so this is likely to vary from company to company and can be extremely complex to build accurately for each shareholder. All the more reason to build the model and make sure everyone agrees it is correct.

Due diligence on VCs

VCs perform due diligence on entrepreneur companies, but all too rarely is the converse the case. There is a feeling that if a VC has the required money and is prepared to invest it on reasonable terms, that is all that is needed. But it's not enough – there are at least two questions that every entrepreneur must ask a VC looking to invest.

Remember a VC works with discrete time-based funds. In the early days of the fund there is strong desire to invest, to put the LPs' money to work. At the other end of a fund's maturity, there is an increasing desire to sell holdings. If multiple VCs are invested in the same company, their different funds' maturities can cause severe problems for an entrepreneur.

So the first due diligence question is: *What is the maturity date for the fund that is investing?* The answer should include the latest point a financial exit can take place for the fund, how much money there remains in the fund (called reserves) and whether there are any allocation limits on investing in each company. In other words, can the investor continue supporting the company to the end?

The second question is harder because it is about people and relationships. The working relationship with the VCs can be anything from good to terrible. A bad relationship might force a strategy change, or prevent the company from raising further investment, or make it impossible for the company to be sold. They might even fire you, the founder CEO, or create an environment where you feel you must or should leave. "Let's bring in someone with more experience"; "You can focus on what you enjoy and are good at"; "You've brought the company this far, let an expert take it to the next level"; "You're not handling this stress well. Let someone else take over" and many similar arguments.

But an incoming CEO is quite likely to raise further investment. In that round, the investors will not necessarily look after the founders' interests. The chances are the founder entrepreneur's wealth will be damaged or even eliminated.

So the second question is: *Can you introduce me to a couple of your existing portfolio companies?* From these conversations you should try and understand what the VC is really interested in (e.g. does the VC want to build a strong standalone company, have a technology play to be sold to a trade buyer, or perhaps merge with another company?); what value-add if any they bring in terms of industry contacts or expertise; how aggressively they interfere with the running of the company; how supportive they are of the CEO and management team; and what the VC's views are about financing terms and generally sharing wealth with the entrepreneur. If you were about to get married, it would be good to speak to some of your partner's old girlfriends or boyfriends if that were possible! You would likely get an honest and perhaps insightful look into your future partner.

Episode 7

MissInge's Share Capital Problem

> There is a realm of time where the goal is not to have but to be, not to own but to give, not to control but to share, not to subdue but to be in accord.
>
> Abraham Joshua Heschel

"Good morning, Dan." Grace welcomes her angel investor into her office. "How are you? Coffee?"

Dan looks at Grace, who seems to be remarkably calm considering the news he recently gave her. How can an entrepreneur who has put so much effort into building her company accept so easily that she will not make anything from the venture?

"Fine thanks. Yes please. Black."

Grace steps over to the coffee machine and starts pressing buttons. She respects Dan and was expecting his news to be bad but she is determined not to get emotional about it. If she has made a mistake with the investment agreements, she will talk to the venture capital investors. They will have to sort something out; after all they need her if MissInge is to be successful. The company can't survive without her, surely. Or can it? That is not something she wants to think about right now – just get to the facts of what the problem is.

With her back to Dan she asks lightly but with a hint of stress in her voice, "So what's wrong with the investment agreements?"

"Grace, it's not really a question of what's wrong with the investment agreements. There's no error as such, it's just that the agreement is very investor–friendly. As you know, there have been a few hiccups in the development of the company which they have used to their advantage. But let me start at the beginning, because it is a little complex."

Dan stands up and heads for the whiteboard, marker in hand.

"The most likely outcome for MissInge is a trade sale either to one of the big fashion brands looking to get into your market niche, or to one of your competitors. It's less likely that you'll list the shares on a stock market through an IPO because you would probably need to be a larger, more general fashion company, although that remains an option. So let's assume it's a trade sale."

"Most deals are done 'cash and debt free' meaning that the seller is responsible for paying off any loans the company has but gets to keep any cash the company has in its balance sheet."

"Then the investor liquidation preferences are paid together with any accrued interest or dividends. Any remaining funds are then distributed equally to all shareholders. You do understand liquidation preferences I think? We've discussed them before."

"Yes, I think so. In our case, don't you mean the investors get paid twice? They get their investment back through the liquidation preference and they get a percentage of the company?" asks Grace.

"I'm afraid so, yes. Probably most VC investments at the moment are participating liquidation preferences. All of that has to be paid off before the ordinary shares are worth anything."

"Let's go through MissInge's balance sheet to see what would happen if the company is sold," continues Dan. "It's easiest to work through real numbers, so let's assume you sell at the end of next year for €15 million. I personally think that would be a great price to get for a company with less than €11 million of sales."

"Freycinet Fashions was sold for three times revenue, just last month. We shouldn't accept anything less," retorts Grace.

"But the buyer was desperate as I remember it. Wasn't Freycinet eating their lunch? It was sold for much more than anyone expected and you can't assume you would be able to get such a premium for MissInge. It would be nice but let's be more down to earth with this example."

"OK, but I'm not going to sell the company for any price."

"Let's do the analysis. First, the debt in MissInge has to be repaid. You have a €1 million soft loan from that quasi–government agency as start–up help. Adding on interest of about €150,000 that will have accrued by the end of the year brings the total to €1.15 million."

"You have had €6 million of VC investment so far, so €7 million with the round extension, all on the basis of participating 1x liquidation preferences. So that needs to be paid off next." Dan is in full flow now.

"There are accrued dividends to be paid on the investor shares which, as they were invested at different times, are harder to work out. The dividend rate is 10 per cent per annum and I estimate the total to be €1.5 million. That's the figure to the end of next year; its actual value depends on when you sell the company. It would of course be higher if you sell next year or the year after."

"Higher by how much?"

"By 10 per cent of €7 million, or €700,000 per year. You have to increase the value of the company by that amount each year just to stand still on the valuation. At least it doesn't compound each year – the figure stays the same."

"It might be easier to look at all this in some tables I have prepared," says Dan, handing Grace some papers. "These are the cumulative euro investment amounts, including the new round:"

Invested €000	2007	2008	2009	2010	2011	2012	2013
Grace Inge	50	50	50	50	50	50	50
Dan Rossi	300	300	300	300	300	300	300
Investors	0	2,000	6,000	7,000	7,000	7,000	7,000
Total invested €000	350	2,350	6,350	7,350	7,350	7,350	7,350

"It shows the €300,000 I invested alongside your €50,000 to get the company started in 2007. We've raised two rounds of VC funding, €2 million in 2008 and another €4 million in 2009, the latter at a much higher valuation."

"And these," continues Dan, "are the ownership and valuation tables. As you know, the offer for the additional €1 million is at the valuation of the 2008 round. The argument is that you should have raised enough in the first place and investing the extra is not something they welcome."

Ownership %	2007	2008	2009	2010
Grace Inge	60%	34%	25%	15%
Dan Rossi	40%	23%	17%	10%
Investors	0%	29%	43%	60%
Employee option pool		15%	15%	15%
Post–money valuation €000	750	7,000	27,094	6,000
Pre–money valuation €000	450	5,000	23,094	5,000

"The post–money valuation is the amount invested divided by the percentage of the company they receive. In the latest round, for example, the investors will get 20 per cent more of the company for €1 million – so the post–money valuation is €5 million."

"And the pre–money valuation is just the post–money less the amount invested," suggests Grace.

"Yes – it represents the value of the company before the investment is made," says Dan.

"After the latest round, you will own 15 per cent and I will own 10 per cent. All the calculations are done 'fully diluted,' meaning they take into account employee options plus anything else that is not actually part of the share capital at the moment. We now build an exit model, calculating how much each will get if the company is sold."

"Go on."

Dan takes a breath and hands Grace another piece of paper.

"Here's the summary," Dan says. "It assumes the company is sold at the end of 2011 for €15 million."

Sale proceeds		€ 15,000,000
Debt + interest	−€ 1,156,000	
Liquidation prefs	−€ 7,000,000	
Dividends	−€ 1,500,000	
Total	−€ 9,656,000	−€ 9,656,000
Shareholders get		€ 5,344,000

"The transaction costs – lawyers, bankers, etc. – need to come off that figure. Let's assume that leaves €5 million to be distributed. You would receive €750,000 for your 15% and I would get €500,000 for my 10%. That's not much of a return considering the effort that has gone into building the company." Dan sits down, waiting for Grace to react.

"It also means the option holders get very little. A senior person such as Joe with about 1 per cent of the equity will get a few tens of thousands of euros – hardly life–changing," says Grace grimly. "How much does the situation improve if the company is sold for more, such as €25 million?" asks Grace.

"Not as much as you might hope. I prepared a table for various exit values." Dan passes Grace another piece of paper.

Exit valuations €000		€ 15,000	€ 20,000	€ 25,000
Liquidation prefs	1x	–7,000	–7,000	–7,000
Debt		–1,156	–1,156	–1,156
Accrued dividends		–1,500	–1,500	–1,500
To shareholders		5,344	10,344	15,344
Grace Inge	15%	802	1,552	2,302
Dan Rossi	10%	534	1,034	1,534
Employee option pool	15%	802	1,552	2,302
Investors	60%	3,207	6,207	9,207
Investors total		11,707	14,707	17,707
Grace Inge		5%	8%	9%
Investors total in %		78%	74%	71%

"Even if you sell the company for €25 million, which would be a tremendous achievement, the investors still get 71 per cent of the economic value."

"Thank you, Dan. I now see what you mean, although I can't say I like it. What do you think I should do? Can I get the shareholders to change the liquidation preferences or to forgo their dividends do you think?"

"As far as the whole structure is concerned, I honestly think you're stuffed, Grace. The investors have investment committees and such a change would need to be presented to their committee and why should they agree to a change? The time to have done that was at the time of the initial investment. The only thing we can do is get the best possible deal in the current round."

"What is the deal and how can we improve it?"

"As I mentioned, they are offering to invest at the pre–money valuation of the round before last. That's a little unfair and perhaps opportunistic, so we should clearly try and get them to invest at a higher valuation. But there is in fact a much bigger problem: the anti–dilution protection."

"This isn't some legal mumbo jumbo, Grace," Dan continues, "it could mean the investors ending up with much more of the company than even the figures we've just discussed. Look at this section of the original term sheet under which the VCs invested." Dan passes Grace a photocopy and points to a particular paragraph.

"Remember that the current term sheet just says that all terms will be the same as the last round, so this clause applies, on the face of it at least."

Grace picks it up and starts to read.

Anti–dilution protection:	The Investment is subject to a full ratchet adjustment to prevent dilution if the Company issues additional equity capital at any time in the future at a purchase price lower than the Conversion Price, except for equity capital issued in connection with an employee stock option plan (a "Down Round"). In the event of a future Down Round, the Company will issue sufficient additional shares to Investor at no charge as if Investment had been made at the Down Round price. The Conversion Price is adjusted for proportional adjustment to stock splits, stock dividends, recapitalizations and similar issuances of equity capital.

"And you think this counts as a down round, do you?" asks Grace.

"I don't see why not."

"What would be the effect on their shareholding?"

"It would be extremely bad. They invested €4 million, so at the proposed pre–money valuation of €5 million they would be entitled to 4/5, or 80 per cent of the company. Add in the previous investment and they would pretty much own the whole company."

"But that means that no one would make any money at all. The founders, the staff, no one – how am I going to incentivize them if the company they built turns out to be owned by some bunch of faceless financiers? It is not as if they are adding any value, the board representatives are little more than spotty teenagers for the most part. Tim for example has never run a company, or run anything as far as I'm aware." Grace is getting angrier.

"Grace, I understand your emotional reaction, but don't blame the VC. The time to discuss the terms was when you agreed the deal. Why would they change anything now?"

"I could threaten to leave. Then where would they be?"

"That is very dangerous talk – you would be putting your reputation on the line, with the investment community and the public, because you are not prepared to stick to an agreement. My advice is not to make that threat to anyone outside this room, certainly not to the VCs or the board."

"So what do I do? Put this whole venture down to experience and hope the next one actually makes me some money? I have put my heart and soul into MissInge and for what? A pat on the back?"

"I'm afraid that is about it, Grace. When you get to the point of selling the company, there may be something that can be done. A carve–out of the investment proceeds for example is quite common in these situations.

The investors know they can't sell the business without management being motivated."

"I don't see how that is different from where I am at the moment. Management needs to be motivated in order to build the company up, so why can't a carve–out be agreed now? How does a carve–out work anyway?"

"A carve–out is when a portion of the sale proceeds is paid to the management of the company separately from their shareholding. The amount varies but it is typically in the range of 5 to 10 per cent. So, taking 10% as an illustration, if the company is sold for €20 million, two would go the management in the form of a bonus and 18 would go to the shareholders. There may be a sliding scale to encourage a sale at the highest possible price. As it is a bonus, it would probably be treated as income for tax purposes, which for many is not as attractive as a capital gain. But there may be something that can be done at the time."

"Well, let's get a carve–out agreed now."

"No, Grace. The investors will not agree to a carve–out until a sale is imminent. The only thing you can do at this stage is to make them aware that you now understand the share structure – that you are not likely to make a capital gain from the sale of the business. Otherwise all we can do is work on the terms of the current round."

"Do the investors know the shares are not worth anything?"

"Of course. You might ask them to approve an increase to your pay package, or to get some share options."

"But options are not worth anything much, that's your whole point."

"They would be worth something if the company is sold for a lot more than €20 million. In any case, making the investors aware that you finally understand the share cap table is a good idea. Let's see what comes out of it – just don't expect a miracle."

"I'm going to look like a real idiot, if it gets out. I can see the headlines now: 'Entrepreneur of the Year does not understand how shares work'. Won't the investors worry that I'm incompetent?"

"Naive perhaps, but I don't think they would call you incompetent. You would be surprised Grace, but most entrepreneurs don't understand shares and options. Investors understand that entrepreneurs and their team need to be kept motivated and that remains your best and perhaps only trump card. You also need to educate the management team too – that's only fair."

"All right, I will, but I'm not at all happy about this, Dan. I think someone should have gone through this when we took in the investment. Perhaps our lawyers, or even you."

"Point taken, I should have looked at this in some detail earlier but I was not really involved in the negotiations at the time. As you know, I am not a board member and all the discussions took place at the board level, in other words between you and the investors."

"Dan, I really need your help, if nothing else to balance the investors and to make sure we work for the benefit of the company and not just for the investors. Would you be prepared to join the board, perhaps as chairman? I know the investors like you and they have been talking about boosting the board."

"Grace, I would like that very much. I am really excited about MissInge and would love to spend more time on it. Why don't you suggest that to the investors and let me know?"

Dan takes a breath and continues, "As far as the last round investment is concerned, I'm sorry, but we are where we are. Let's try and make the best of the current round. Let's see whether they might waive the anti–dilution right for this round and invest at a higher valuation than they are offering."

"Thank you, Dan, that's helpful and appreciated. I will go and break the bad news to the team."

From: Grace Inge
Sent: 24 October 2009 15:07
To: Dan Rossi
cc: "MissInge board"

Subject: Board

Dan,

I'm really pleased to confirm that the board has invited you to join as chairman. Let's sit down when you have a moment and discuss terms. I am very much looking forward to working with you – there is so much going on!
Grace Inge

CEO
MissInge Fashions

From: Dan Rossi
Sent: 28 October 2009 12:35
To: Grace Inge

Subject: Board and Investment

Hi Grace,

Thank you for the opportunity to serve as chairman – the agreement is signed and in the mail.
I have spent quite some time with the investors on the current round. They have agreed to waive the anti–dilution provisions for the current round, but they will not budge on the valuation.

Dan

From: Joe Santos
Sent: 15 November 2009 23:15
To: Grace Inge

Subject: Options

Grace,

Thanks for explaining how the share options work as well as the whole investment structure. I finally feel I understand what is going on, although I would really like to have understood it a lot earlier. I get the impression you would have liked to have understood it earlier too.

MissInge is a great company and you are a terrific boss to work for, but as you know I am really short of cash since my divorce. I need this job to bring in a big capital return for me so that I can pay down some of the insane mortgage on my tiny apartment.

I now understand that there is little hope of making much, if anything. So I'm really sorry, but I am resigning from MissInge. I will see the year out and leave then.

Please don't take this personally.

Best regards,
Joe Santos
VP Sales
MissInge Fashions

Chapter 7
Options and Shares

Make happy those who are near, and those that are far will come.

Chinese proverb

An option gives you the right to buy a share at today's price some time in the future. If in the future the share is worth more than it is today, you make money. If it is worth less, you don't exercise the option, so you don't lose money. If the company becomes extremely successful, you can make lots of money for no investment of your own. The value created as a start–up grows and prospers is shared across the team of people who build the company.

Options are granted to motivate key staff members who join a start–up after the founders. The possibility of a large reward helps create an entrepreneurial culture, encouraging employees to work harder for less job security and often lower pay than in a more established company.

Particularly in the run–up to the Internet bubble in the early 2000s, there were many stories of even junior staff making fortunes in technology companies such as Yahoo, Apple, Microsoft, Intel and Oracle. But if a company is less successful than everyone hopes and expects, employees find out that their options are worthless despite many years of hard work, perhaps at relatively low pay.

Contrary to what some people think, granting options did not die out when the bubble burst, and granting options is still a common employee incentive for start–up companies. However, options are often misunderstood by staff and not structured as well as they could be by the entrepreneur.

Part of the source of the employee's confusion comes from the sheer flexibility of shares. For example, consider someone looking to decide which of two companies to join. They are identical in all respects other than their number of shares. One company is set up with 1,000 shares and the other with 10,000. The prospective employee is being offered options over 1 per cent of the share capital in each, meaning he would have ten options in the first company and

100 options in the second. The perception of many is that the second company is being more generous because it is offering more options and he would opt to join that company. The total value of the options is of course identical in each case.

Investors normally determine the percentage of the company that can be granted in options, as too many options would dilute the value of their investment. In the survey, 56 per cent of companies allot between 6 per cent and 10 per cent of the company to share options, and 37 per cent of companies allot between 11 per cent and 15 per cent. In the US, this figure may very well be higher. A good starting point in discussions with investors is to allow a share option pool of 15 per cent of the company's shares.

Having created the pool of options, the rules and structure of the option scheme will depend very much on local legislation. Independent of where the company is located, options generally have the following terms:

Life

The option is valid for a certain finite term at the end of which the option expires. This might be ten years for example. Options are also normally cancelled when an employee leaves the company, and exercise or cancellation is compulsory in events such as the company being acquired, or an IPO.

Exercise price

This is the price at which the share can be bought, which is normally the market value of the share at the time of the grant of the option. During the life of the option, a share can be bought at the exercise price. Many countries have favourable tax treatments for options and the relevant tax authority may need to approve the exercise price. The market price of the shares could be set to the valuation at the last round of investment, or the price at which shares have most recently changed hands, or an independent valuation by an expert. The market value of shares is normally very much lower than the investor pays, because of the liquidation preferences and other investor privileges.

Perhaps within a relatively short time period a new investor has bought shares at €1 each; shares have recently been sold by one existing shareholder to another for €0.75 each and the company's accountant has valued the shares as being worth €0.50 each. The market price could be any of these prices. It is important to set the exercise price as low as possible to maximize the return to the option holder and to remember that the price per share will be much lower than the amount an investor pays or has paid. When a company is sold, employee options are exercised and the resulting shares sold.

Vesting

This means that not all the options that have been granted are immediately available for exercise. They have to be earned. This varies from company to company but might for example be over 4 years. That means that each month, 1/48 of the options become available for exercise (often there is no vesting in the first year, meaning 12/48 vest on the first anniversary). If the company is sold 24 months after the options are granted to an individual for example, he can only exercise half his options.

Other rights

It is usual for options to be cancelled when an employee leaves the company. This is to ensure that the option pool is focused on the group of people who are growing the business.

Options do not carry the same rights as shares, for example to dividends, access to the company's shareholder meetings or the right to vote. They also do not have anti–dilution or pre–emption rights, meaning the option holder is not entitled to more options in the event of a capital increase, fundraising, or other increase in the number of shares.

However, it is common for the option pool to be increased at each fundraising and that should be a standard part of the negotiations with VC.

Exercise

It may make sense to limit option exercise to the point of the sale of the company or other liquidity event such as an IPO.

A cashless exercise mechanism is very desirable, enabling option holders to exercise the options, sell the shares and receive the net proceeds. This avoids the problem of the option holder finding the cash to pay for the shares and taking a risk on the sale price, which is especially important if the two figures are very close. This is particularly relevant when the shares are listed on an exchange and the price fluctuates.

Options in the mix of an employee package

Options are the highest risk element in an employment package. It could have no value, or a lot. And it could achieve that value this year, or in five years, or never.

A bonus or other kind of variable compensation has a lower potential value than options and is less but still risky. For example, the company may predict doubling sales in a year. If growth is only 50 per cent in that year, which is still an excellent achievement, no bonus is likely.

Salary on the other hand is relatively large and arrives every month without fail. It is low risk, high reward. The salary bill is also in most start–ups the single largest cost item.

Employee benefits, such as a company car, are generally of lower value (because they are normally worth less than the salary) and low risk because like salary they arrive reliably every month.

Understanding an employee's desire for risk and financial priorities is the key to designing a package that will attract and retain them.

Shares vs options

Some employees will ask for shares rather than options, perhaps because they have had bad experiences with options, working hard for several years for a company only to find there is no payment at the end.

There are three possible sources of dissatisfaction with options:

1. Options need to be exercised, so if the company is bought for a relatively low price, it may make the options worthless.
2. Options expire, for example when an employee leaves the company, whereas shares do not.
3. Shares feel more real, in that the shareholder can take part in annual shareholder meetings and vote, and they receive annual accounts and other shareholder correspondence.

In fact, it is preferable to issue options rather than shares to staff. If a shareholder leaves the company and retains his shares, they are benefiting from the increase in value in the shares from the work of others, without putting any work in themselves. Consider a company with four founders, each with 25 per cent of the business. If three were to leave and the remaining founder continues to build the company until it is sold, 75 per cent of the value he creates through his efforts would go to people outside the business.

As an entrepreneur, you will probably want to have the right to get the shares back when a co-founder leaves, and to set up an option scheme for employees rather than allow them to buy shares. If someone leaves and for whatever reason you want them to remain a shareholder, this can be achieved by allowing them to exercise some of their options.

If there are several founders of a business, there should be a shareholder agreement covering what happens to the shares of founders who leave. It is common for at least some of the shares of the leaving founder to be sold or transferred to the remaining founder or founders. This is often governed by whether the founder or employee is a 'good' or 'bad' leaver, however that is defined. A good leaver for example might be someone who is made redundant or can no longer work because of illness. A bad leaver might be someone who resigns.

The price could either be the market value of the shares at the time of leaving, either agreed by the parties or set by an independent expert, or at a fixed price, such as fixed premium over the original price paid for the shares.

Instead of being bought by the remaining entrepreneur, it may be possible for the shares to be bought by the company itself, which has the effect of increasing the percentage ownership of all the remaining share and option holders.

Episode 8

Keeping Joe on Board

Trust me, I'm a salesman.

Sales motto

From: Grace Inge
Sent: 16 November 2009 08:15
To: Joe Santos
Subject: Re: Options

Joe,

You're up late, so this is clearly occupying your mind. I think you are making the wrong decision; let me explain why.

It is true that your options would not be worth much if MissInge is sold today for €20 million or less. But the company is not up for sale and I am <u>much more ambitious than that</u>. We have caught the imagination of the fashion industry with our designs and there is a lot more in the pipeline, as you know. We are on the crest of a wave and we need to ride it for as long and for as far as we can. This is not the time to quit!

The company has made great progress in sorting out its recent financial problems to the point where I think the supply shortages we have suffered from, which have affected your ability to make sales and of course commission income, are behind us and we will be able to grow at a faster rate. According to my calculations you could end up earning more than me this year from your sales commissions, because sales are so over-plan. Would you have the same earning power at a new company?

I will speak to the board to see whether we can address the problem of the exercise price of your options. As you know, it is not easy to change the price but we may be able to do something.

Joe, I need you to be driving the sales forward and not worrying about this. Please reconsider your resignation.

Best regards,

Grace Inge
CEO
MissInge Fashions

From: Joe Santos
Sent: 16 November 2009 09:15
To: Grace Inge
Subject: Re: Options

Grace,

You are right that this is of great concern to me. Half my money seems to go to my ex and half to the tax authorities, a cycle I need to break.

I am really pleased you think the inventory problem has been solved – I saw the recent announcement about Mary and her team leaving the company as part of the outsourcing deal you've signed so I imagine it is to do with that. I could certainly do with the extra commission and have no problems earning more than you!

OK – I will suspend my resignation until you can see what can be done with the board. But I really need them and you to come through with something spectacular for me to stay, so we are not home and dry yet.

As you know, this is nothing to do with you or with MissInge's products. I just need some way forward financially.

Best regards,

Joe Santos
VP Sales
MissInge Fashions

From: Grace Inge
Sent: 24 November 2009 15:03
To: Joe Santos
Subject: Re: Options

Joe,

The board has agreed to re-price your options. Let's talk.

Grace Inge

CEO
MissInge Fashions

From: Joe Santos
Sent: 26 November 2009 08:07
To: Grace Inge
Subject: Re: Options

Grace,

Thanks for the talk yesterday. I have thought it over overnight as you suggested and wanted you to know that I have decided to stay with the company.

Having the options re-priced to a point where I will start to make money as soon as the company's sales price exceeds €20 million makes a huge difference and I agree that we should set our sights much higher. This is a great company and if someone buys it for such a small amount, I think it would be like theft.

I also appreciate the model you produced for me showing the value of my expected sales commissions at the new higher sales forecast levels. They will make a huge difference to me.

Thanks for your understanding as we worked through this.

Best regards,

Joe Santos
VP Sales
MissInge Fashions

From: Grace Inge
Sent: 26 November 2009 08:10
To: Joe Santos
Subject: Re: Options

Joe,

You're welcome. Good luck and good selling!

Grace Inge

CEO
MissInge Fashions

Grace leans back from her PC, pleased that the Joe issue has been solved. Her mobile rings.

"Is that Grace Inge?"

"Yes, who is this?"

"My name is Mike Bergbloom from Guggenstein Associates. We are an investment bank based in New York."

"I'm sorry, but I'm not sure how you got my phone number. I imagine you are trying to sell me something and I doubt very much I'm interested. Please call my office if you want to talk to me and I would ask you not to use my mobile number again."

"Just a moment, let me explain. I am not trying to sell you anything. Guggenstein Associates has been retained to advise a large multinational company on possible acquisition targets. Your firm's name has come up and I wanted to see if you were open to a discussion."

"Oh. Go on."

"We are advising one of the major global fashion brands on growth strategy by acquisition. The objective is to locate the right companies that could benefit from our client's global reach, low-cost manufacturing, supply chain skills and international sales channels. MissInge's name came up because of your strong brand and product innovation skills. Those are just the sort of attributes our client is seeking."

"Who is your client?"

"I'm sorry, but I can only divulge that after we have signed a non-disclosure agreement. I can assure you that you will have heard of the company and that they have the financial wherewithal for an all-cash offer. My question stands, is this something MissInge might be interested in discussing?"

Grace pauses for a moment. This is so completely unexpected, being phoned up by an investment banker from the other side of the world. She wonders whether Mike is sitting in a large tinted-glass corner office on the umpteenth floor of a large skyscraper. In previous times he might have been puffing on a large cigar. This could be a really interesting opportunity, but she needs to be careful not to blow it so she chooses her words carefully.

"Well...Mr Bergbloom, was it?"

"Yes, call me Mike."

"And call me Grace. Mike, MissInge is not for sale."

"Think of us like a headhunter, Grace. We identify targets and our clients pay a premium precisely because the targets are not for sale."

"I see. So you understand I cannot tell you whether we are open to a discussion at this point as our focus is on growing the business. In any case I would need to talk to the board as there are outside investors."

"Yes, I know."

Grace wondered what else Guggenstein Associates knew about her and MissInge. It wasn't a very comforting thought. Nor a productive one at this moment. With a slight shudder, she came back to the conversation.

"OK, Mike. Let's sign the NDA and see what your client has to say to us."

Chapter 8
Valuing a Company

Two is not equal to three, even for very large values of two.

Grabel's law

Entrepreneurs put huge emotional effort into building their companies, so arriving at a valuation is both hard and very personal. An objective valuation, meaning one that is acceptable to a third party, is needed at the very least at the point of an investment and when the business is sold. Valuing a company is difficult, but getting a good price for the business is even harder.

The value of a business is not necessarily the same as the price someone is prepared to pay for it. The valuation is driven by the company's financial numbers, but the price might differ from the valuation for a variety of reasons:

1. Company results: the quality and consistency of the financial results and cash flows, the company's forecasted Cash Flow and industry comparables.
2. Environment: industry outlook, general economic outlook, regulatory climate, country traditions and development; the quality of the management team.
3. Timing: trends in the stock market and in the M&A market; the stage of the company's development, industry cycle.
4. Motives: investors' objectives and timing, management's objectives, pressures on different parties such as competition or even personal; the objectives of strategic vs financial buyers.
5. Process: percentage of the company being sold, the number of truly interested buyers and the ability of the owners to sell the long-term potential of the business.

Sometimes an acquirer is prepared to pay more than the economic value – a strategic premium – when the acquirer expects advantages from combining the companies. This might be in the form of cost synergies, where costs can be reduced from combining companies through the elimination of overlaps, or product and sales synergies, where sales can be increased by sharing technology or products and by selling to each other's customers.

A strategic premium can be paid for more esoteric reasons such as helping the buyer improve other parts of his business, or to prevent a competitor having access to the technology or simply because they are playing a larger game. Suppose you were running a company with annual sales of a billion euros. You spot a small company with some exciting technology that, if built into your product, would increase your sales and profits by 10 per cent. You would be prepared to pay quite a lot for the company, even if the small company had few sales itself.

Every entrepreneur hopes for a "strategic" sale of the business. Unfortunately, as investors do not have such operational synergies, it is rare for an investor to pay a strategic premium. But investors and acquirers use the same techniques to value a company, even if gut feelings, rules of thumb, competition and common sense are often more important than scientific methods. This is especially true for very early stage companies, where there are fewer numbers on which to base a scientific valuation. An experienced angel or VC would say that no early stage company is worth more than about €3 million. In some cases this may be far lower.

An objective valuation – as opposed to the entrepreneur's subjective view – is never one exact number but a range based on market data (the market valuation) and on the forecasted internally generated cash flows (the intrinsic valuation).

A market valuation uses ratios from other companies, private and public, and multiplies these together with the company's revenue, profit or cash flow. If the benchmark company is listed, the valuation is obviously the number of shares times the market price of the shares. Private companies are benchmarked at the time of an investment round and when they are sold.

The intrinsic valuation is based on the Discounted Cash Flow of the company.

Let's start with the method most commonly used by VCs.

Venture capital method

This method is a blend of common sense and logic.

The way it works is to set a desired multiple of the investment, along the lines of "I want to make a return of at least 10x my investment". The logic behind this method is that, in the VC world, investment times are short and required returns are high, so whether an investment exits in three years or in five years does not make a material difference to the investor. It also reflects the reality that estimating when a company is going to exit is extremely hard – companies are more often sold when someone wants to buy them rather than when they meet a particular milestone.

The exit price is estimated at the time of investment by looking at the values of similar listed companies or the prices at which similar companies have been sold.

Together the amount invested, the desired return and the estimated exit price give a percentage of the company that a VC needs to own.

Take the hypothetical example of an investor looking to invest €3 million in a company. In three years the company is expected to have revenues of €10 million, which would be a good time to sell the business. Similar companies have recently been changing hands at a valuation of 5x revenue, implying an exit valuation for the company of €50 million. If the VC wants to make a 5x return on his investment, the VC expects €15 million (5x €3 million) at exit, equivalent to 30 per cent of the equity at exit. Assuming no dilution, the company would be valued today at €10 million, being the €3 million investment divided by the 30 per cent.

This method is the most common valuation technique used by VCs, especially for early stage businesses. As you might expect, the survey indicated that multiples are much higher for earlier stage companies, to reflect both the higher level of risk and the longer time before the exit or liquidity event:

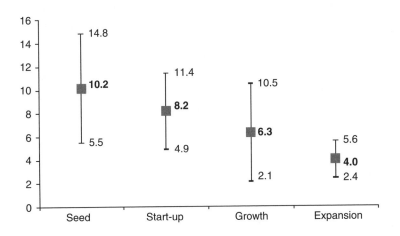

Elsewhere in the survey, VCs stated the goal of achieving 3x the value of their fund, which appears at odds with the above multiples. Why do they require 4x to 10x return from the investments when they are only looking to achieve 3x fund return? The answer lies mainly in portfolio considerations: the financial performance of the successful companies have to offset the poor returns and losses from the living dead. Multiples are reduced in future investment rounds, because more is being invested probably without significantly changing the exit valuation.

Multiples method

This method uses multiples, normally of revenue, or, for later stage profitable companies, of profits. So, for example, you work out the valuation of comparable companies as a multiple of their revenue. Applying that multiple to the company you want to value gives you its value.

In listed shares, the most common multiple is the Price/Earnings ratio. In very early stage companies with low or no revenues, it might be a multiple of the sales pipeline or even "eyeballs" for web companies. An example might be an Internet business that is focused on building brand and users, and does not yet have a business model for generating significant revenues. In the early days of the companies Twitter, Facebook and LinkedIn, for example, revenues were modest but there were a large and rapidly growing number of users.

The big difference between this method and the others is that it measures the current value of the business rather than its expected value at the time the VC realizes his investment.

All multiple methods should and will produce a range of valuations, which helps to understand how the market sees the boundaries of possible values for the company. Therefore it is good to consider all possible valuations, not least because the other side is doing the same. However, the problem with multiples is that the companies you use as benchmarks are themselves likely to be very different. Investment bankers can spend a lot of time calculating and adjusting ratios and numbers. For example, if your benchmarks for a sales multiple are derived from the sales of an unlisted company in India with a few million in revenue and the sales of a multibillion US listed company, you might need to apply a discount factor for size, another for country and yet another for listed vs unlisted. Investment bankers can become quite creative and will always produce a believable model, but in the end you may have to question the value created by this exercise.

Cash flow method

Economic value is normally calculated using discounted cash flows (DCF) and is ideal for later stage deals with predictable cash flows. Here the principle is that money is worth more today than it is tomorrow – the so-called time value of money. You would rather have €100 today than €100 in a year's time, even if you don't need the money today. If you have it now, you could invest it and receive interest. If you don't receive the money until next year, you might have to borrow some money to bridge you until you receive the cash.

The return you seek as an investor is the cost of the capital (for a VC, this is the hurdle rate) plus the desired risk-adjusted return from the investment (for a VC, this produces the carry).

The other element that determines the cost of money is the risk. Suppose you are considering an investment of €100 that will return €110 in a year's time. As an alternative, there is an investment that has a 50 per cent chance of returning €120 in a year's time; otherwise it will return €100. On average the two investments are worth the same. You may prefer one over the other, reflecting your appetite for risk. Alternatively the price of one of the investments might need to change to make it equally attractive to the other.

The Discounted Cash Flow method estimates the amount and time point of each cash movement, both an investment (cash out) and each return (cash in). Herein lies the difficulty of this method for early-stage and growth companies, as the actual cash flows will most likely be very different from those forecast (we will raise more concerns about DCF a little later). Today's value of each cash movement is reduced by applying a discount rate, the desired risk adjusted return.

The DCF calculation will produce a positive or negative monetary figure, called the Net Present Value (NPV) of the investment if the initial investment is deducted, or Present Value (PV) without. NPV is the excess value of the investment after the risk has been allowed for, the capital has been paid for and the desired profit made. If the NPV is negative, the investment will not produce the desired return.

In the survey, VCs were asked for the discount rate they use for companies at different stages. As you might expect, discount rates were higher for earlier stage ventures and decreased as companies mature and become lower risk (the data for the seed stage is excluded because of limited responses, which makes sense as DCF is not appropriate for early stage companies):

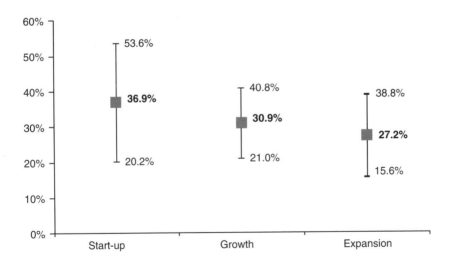

DCF is the way listed shares are valued, in that the price of a share is – theoretically at least – the present value (PV) of all estimated future dividends and capital distributions.

In our interviews we discovered a few VCs using the Monte Carlo method assigns probabilities and ranges, or standard deviations, for each possible outcome of an investment. An investment might fail altogether, or succeed moderately, or very well in introducing a new product, or entering a new market. These various possible outcomes are fed into a computer which runs a few thousand scenarios and produces a result expressed as a statistical significance such as "A 95 per cent chance that the value of the company is €5 million or more". With small young companies, though, the data used is not likely to be very reliable because there are just too many unknowns. So there is a real risk of garbage in, garbage out.

Even though Monte Carlo is not widely used (and arguably is not a suitable method for valuing a young company), it is very important to understand the drivers of Cash Flow and to build several different scenarios in order to estimate future cumulated cash needs. Plotted on a graph, the cash need usually has the shape of "J" and is therefore called a "J curve", an expression that has become quite common. This sensitivity analysis of Cash Flow also helps to understand where to focus the business and its investments cash-wise.

There are two particular problems with DCF in valuing early stage companies:

1. Risk measurement

As the risk is built into the discount rate, the risk premium is applied every year, which can distort the attractiveness of a company that is likely to take longer to develop before it is ready for sale. Consider two companies of equal risk that each requires an investment of €1 million. The VC's investment in Company A is expected to be worth €2 million in two years, while in Company B it is expected to be worth €4 million in 5 years. The companies are early stage, so the discount rate used is from the survey: 36.9 per cent.

€000 in year	0	1	2	3	4	5	NPV@36.9%
Company A	–1,000	0	2,000				49
Company B	–1,000	0	0	0	0	4,000	–123

On this valuation basis, the VC would invest in Company A and not in Company B because the NPV from B is negative, meaning that it did not meet the investment criteria.

Suppose that the discount rate breaks down as 10 per cent hurdle rate – the rate the VC has to pay the LP investor, 6.9 per cent for the VC's carry and 20 per cent for the risk. As the risk is identical for both companies, it can be removed to compare the relative attractiveness of investing in each company. Using the new discount rate of 16.9 per cent, the situation looks very different:

€000 in Year	0	1	2	3	4	5	NPV@16.9%
Company A	−1,000	0	2,000				397
Company B	−1,000	0	0	0	0	4,000	712

Here in contrast the VC would invest in both companies, but would prefer to invest in Company B.

Considering how much was earned per euro invested – the multiples method – it becomes even more obvious: Company A makes 2x and Company B 4x. This is also one of the reasons why VCs use both methods, and why they prefer the multiples method.

2. Future rounds of investment

Most companies need more than one round of investment, yet at the time of each investment further funding is not necessarily assumed to be needed and if it is, when and how large future rounds will be is not clear. As DCF requires all the cash flows – in and out – to be modelled, it is very hard to build an accurate DCF model for multiple rounds of investment.

There are so many factors that can change every single Cash Flow, that to make investment decisions about early-stage companies based on DCF alone is a little strange, and, many experienced investors would say, useless.

Minimum return method

VCs have limited capacity to watch over a large number of investments at any one time. As a result they may decide – independent of the multiples or DCF of an investment – to set a monetary threshold for investments, along the lines of "every investment must be capable of providing a return of at least €2 million".

Although this technique is not commonly used by the investors that were polled, with only 23 per cent requiring a minimum return, the fact is that relatively few VC firms invest in early stage companies when the amount to be invested is small. So in a way there is a tacit minimum return.

Taking future rounds into account

The survey confirms how hard it is to predict how much more investment a company will need and how to build it into the investment model. Appendix 2 contains detailed investor comments, which show the variety of views but a lack of a common method.

Perhaps the most usual is that each investment is looked at on its own merits and is expected to be justified by itself, as a standalone investment. This is one of the reasons why down-rounds are relatively common.

Using multiple methods

In reality, most VCs use several methods to decide the range of valuations of a company and, more importantly, whether they want to invest at all.

Exit multiples are the most common way of valuing companies at any stage of development. As you might expect, the survey showed an increasing use of DCF and multiples as companies mature. Thankfully, perhaps, Monte Carlo analysis is not widely used at all.

Acquisition valuations

Acquirers look at the effect the acquisition will have on its own company metrics, which are usually earnings per share (EPS). If an acquisition is expected to reduce EPS, it is called "dilutive", whereas if it is expected to increase EPS it is called "accretive". An acquiring company will take into account any synergies in the transaction such as a reduction in costs or an increase in sales that are not in the business plan of the business being acquired. This can mean that an acquiring company that is listed is willing to pay a different amount for a company than one might expect just by looking at the acquisition target by itself.

The value of a company is not reflected anywhere on the balance sheet. The equity of the company, calculated as assets minus liabilities, is called the "book value", but is not the same as what someone would be prepared to pay for the business. The book value is also called the net asset value (NAV).

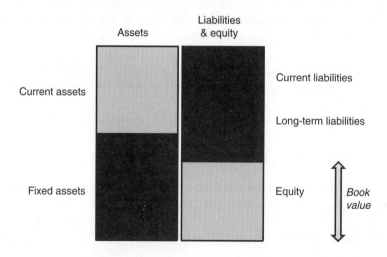

If a company is sold for its book value, it means the business in terms of its customers, brand reputation, market presence, technology and products – once the assets are converted into cash and the debts are repaid – has no value.

In fact a buyer will generally not pay anything for the book value unless it includes items not needed for the business, such as buildings. It is easier to see why if we revert to a simplified balance sheet showing its NFO:

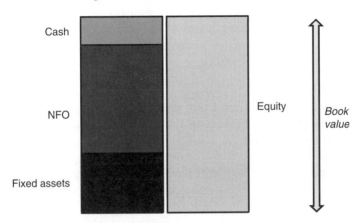

The fixed assets and the NFO are the assets the business needs day to day – as they are locked up in the business, they have no value unless the company is being liquidated. But if the company can reduce its NFO (or its fixed assets) in the run up to being sold, any cash that is released will be kept by the seller.

The price paid by a buyer is the economic value of the business, plus any strategic premium, plus any surplus cash (and less any debt in the business). This is called the enterprise value (EV) and is widely used for private and public valuations. The formula to relate EV to the proceeds the shareholders receive on the sale of the business is simple:

proceeds = enterprise value + cash − debt

That is called a cash and debt free transaction and is the most common way transactions are structured. This is particularly important if the company has a large amount of cash or debt – these belong to the shareholders, not to the acquirer.

How much are the shares worth?

The complex nature of VC investments with its multiple privileges and the cash and debt free method acquisition makes relating the acquisition valuation to the actual value of a share quite complex. Here's how to do it.

1. Deduct the transaction costs

The actual cash receipts need to take into account adviser fees.

net proceeds = price paid − transaction costs

For example, consider a company that had sales last year of €1.5 million. Similar companies have sold for 4x the revenue of the previous year, or €6 million. The investment bank wants €500,000 for selling the company and the lawyers and accountants will charge €200,000. The net proceeds in this example are therefore €5.3 million.

2. Add cash, subtract debt

For a cash and debt free transaction there will be an agreed closing balance sheet. Any surplus cash belongs to the seller and remaining debts are the responsibility of the seller:

cash and debt free proceeds = net proceeds + cash − (debt + interest + redemption premium)

A redemption premium is a way of increasing the return to the loan providers. For example, if €100 is borrowed and the redemption premium is 100 per cent, €200 capital must be repaid (plus the interest). There are other names used, such as underwriting premium, which are all devices to achieve the same effect of increasing the capital to be paid back to the loan provider.

Suppose the company in the above example has a five-month-old €250,000 bridge loan from its investors, with an interest rate of 2 per cent per month and a redemption premium of 50%. There is no cash. The debt is €400,000 (€250,000 + 50% = €375,000, plus €5,000 interest a month for five months). This reduces proceeds to €4.9 million:

cash and debt free proceeds = €5.3 million − €400,000 = €4.9 million

3. Deduct liquidation preferences, accrued dividends and other share privileges.

The company raised €2 million in equity investment, with 1x liquidation preferences, for 40 per cent of the company. There is no provision for dividends.

proceeds to common shareholders = cash and debt free proceeds − share privileges

proceeds to common shareholders = €4.9 million − €2 million = €2.9 million

4. Add proceeds from option exercise

If the share price resulting from the above calculation is higher than the exercise price of the options, it becomes worthwhile for staff to exercise their share options, and the proceeds then need to be added. Suppose in our example there are 900,000 shares in issue and 100,000 options. We know the investors bought 40 per cent of the company – or 400,000 shares – for €2 million, equivalent to €5 a share. A lower option exercise price was agreed, at €1 per share.

The option exercise brings in another €100,000, taking the proceeds to €3 million, or €3 per share, so the option holders will receive €300,000 after they have paid €100,000 to exercise the options.

5. Calculate the proceeds for each shareholder

In this relatively simple example, there are three shareholders or shareholder groups: the founders, the investors and the staff who have options. The proceeds are as follows:

€	Founders	Investors	Staff	Total
Debt		400,000		400,000
Liq. prefs		2,000,000		2,000,000
Shares	1,500,000	1,200,000	300,000	3,000,000
Proceeds	1,500,000	3,600,000	300,000	5,400,000

The proceeds of €5.4 million are made up of the net proceeds of €5.3 million plus the €100,000 from the option exercise.

The profit is calculated by subtracting the cost of the VC's €2 million investment, €250,000 of debt and the €100,000 from the staff option exercise:

€	Founders	Investors	Staff	Total
Proceeds	1,500,000	3,600,000	300,000	5,400,000
Cost	0	2,250,000	100,000	2,350,000
Profit	1,500,000	1,350,000	200,000	3,050,000

(This assumes the founders did not pay anything for their shares.)

6. Conclusions

The founders make a profit of €1.5 million, which may or may not be satisfactory in their eyes.

The investors make €1.35 million net gain from an investment of €2.25 million. This is probably above the fund hurdle rate, so there will be some carry for the partners of the VC firm, provided the rest of the fund achieves the hurdle rate. It would probably not have met their investment targets and interestingly there is a loss made on their common shares (they bought them for €5 each and sold them for €3). The profit comes from the liquidation preferences and the debt structure.

It does not look that attractive for the option holders: they get to share a profit of just €200,000.

Episode 9

The Deal Runs into Trouble

Never give in. Never, never, never, never.

Winston Churchill

The conference phone rings and Grace presses the Call button to answer it.

"Grace? This is Mike Bergbloom from New York. How are you doing today?"

"Yes hi, Mike, this is Grace. I am here with my Chairman, Dan Rossi. We're fine, thank you."

"Hello, Mike. It's good to talk to you again." Dan echoes the welcome.

"Great," says Mike. "I'm here with my usual team. So let's get started. Have you guys got the offer I sent over? The main purpose today is to go through it and make sure you understand what it is, and what it is not."

"Yes, we have it," confirms Grace. "We really want to understand the offer rather than necessarily provide you with feedback today, Mike, if that's OK."

"That's fine. You have a great company, Grace, you know that. My client thinks MissInge Fashions is an attractive asset which would fit in very well with its existing portfolio. We're conscious that this is the first year of profitability and it is on the back of some pretty chunky losses in previous years. That's always the danger with fast-growing companies – if the growth slows down we find a year or two out that we have overpaid. It's very important for our client that the deal is accretive at least in the second year. The stockholders would really punish the company if that turns out not to be the case."

"So we've worked hard to put together a deal that's really attractive to your founders and investors, while being something our stockholders will live with. We believe we understand the dynamics around your investors and we have tried to put in place a package that's interesting for everyone. In particular we've taken into account the need for as much cash to be paid up front – I guess that's a demand from your investors."

"*First point*: our client will offer a package worth up to €22.5 million, with €12.5 million being paid on closing. The remaining €10 million will be placed in an escrow account to be paid out on the 12-month anniversary of the deal, in full if the sales targets have been met and there are no skeletons in the closet. Otherwise the amount would be reduced pro rata."

Mike pauses for a second to let it sink in, before carrying on.

"We require you, Grace, plus some other key members of the management team, to enter into new service agreements. You would be Vice President and General Manager responsible for the MissInge brand, reporting to the Global Executive Vice President, Products. Your compensation will be the same as the other GMs, which is about a 50 per cent increase over your current pay and benefits. In addition, you and the other key management team members will be entitled to a retention bonus equivalent to two months' pay, payable at the same time as the escrow is released. Questions?"

"How do you envisage the escrow working?" Dan asks as Grace is busy taking notes, as well as drawing a circle round the words "50 per cent increase".

"The full amount is paid by us on closing but some of it is held in an escrow account that neither of us can access. We are open to discussing who holds the escrow monies, for example our attorney or a third party. At the end of the earn-out year we produce a statement of sales for the year together with a list of any warranty claims; we agree it with you and the remaining funds are transferred to your shareholders. If we can't agree, we go to arbitration."

"What happens if the sales forecasts are exceeded?" asks Grace.

"Then the maximum €22.5 million is paid. To be honest, sales growth is our greatest concern. We will need to get really comfortable that your sales targets are achievable. We've heard of your problems in Russia, for example."

"What problems in Russia?" asks Grace.

"We understand there are some problems around your launch there. That aside, if you don't make your numbers, or we don't think you will make your numbers while we are trying to close the transaction, this deal is probably going to collapse. Just so we understand each other."

Dan and Grace look at each other. Dan writes "*Russia?*" on his pad. Grace shrugs.

"Is there a break-up fee, so you pay us if you choose to walk away?" asks Dan.

"No break-up fee, no. We're each going to do what we can to make this work and our commitment comes from the effort we're putting into this and the costs we're incurring. My firm is on a success fee, Grace, so trust me, I wouldn't waste your time or mine if I didn't think this deal would go through. But we do require the deal to go exclusive until closing, so that you can't shop the company to anyone else in the meantime."

After a pause, Grace says, "Thanks for all the information and the clarifications, Mike. We'll discuss your offer with the board and the investors, think it over and come back to you soonest."

"Great. I look forward to hearing back from you. Bye for now, Grace. Call me if you need anything."

"Bye, everyone," replies Grace, and hangs up.

"Let's convene the board at once and see what they have to say," says Dan, reaching for the phone.

From: Grace Inge
Sent: 23 March 2010 17:24
To: Mike Bergbloom
Subject: Project Sunflower

Mike,

Please find attached our board's counter-offer. Basically we are looking for a higher cash offer, which we hope very much your client can accommodate.

Best regards,

Grace Inge
CEO
MissInge Fashions

From: Joe Santos
Sent: 26 March 2010 22:16
To: Grace Inge
Subject: Quarterly sales

Grace,

I don't believe this will be a surprise for you, but we are going to miss the quarter's sales targets. I've spent most of the day going through the numbers and "dialling for dollars" – calling our various partners to see if they want any more stock – and I am sure now that we won't achieve the target. I'm really sorry.
The problem has been mainly Russia, which you may not be that familiar with as you and I haven't spoken much in the past few days. You will remember we had to cancel the launch because you needed to go and visit the company interested in buying us. A journalist read this as anti-Russian and wrote a nasty article. Our local distributor got cold feet and cancelled his large launch order.
I also think we have been generally less visible this quarter marketing-wise and again your being so busy hasn't helped.
But I'm not passing the buck – we missed the number and that's my responsibility. I will let you know the final outcome as soon as we close in a couple of days.
Let's get together to come up with a recovery plan for next quarter – I am going to need your help if we are to regain the momentum!

Best regards,

Joe Santos
VP Sales
MissInge Fashions

From: Mike Bergbloom
Sent: 26 March 2010 23:51
To: Grace Inge
Subject: Project Sunflower

Grace,

I have managed to speak to our client today to try and bottom out the issue of valuation, so that you and your investors can make a decision whether to go forward.
Our client remains very interested in MissInge. However, your sales projections are too risky to support the premium pricing you are seeking. To increase our client's current all-cash offer of €22.5 million can only be done by reducing the upfront cash and having a larger portion reserved for the earn-out. We could envisage an offer along the lines of €25 million, but with €10 million up-front and a higher earn-out goal. You'd get the extra only if the company really performed.
If that is something you would like to discuss, let me know and I will set up a call. Just to be clear, my client will not increase the up-front portion of its current offer.

Sincerely,

Mike Bergbloom
Managing Director
Guggenstein Associates

From: Dan Rossi
Sent: 29 March 2010 07:56
To: Grace Inge
Subject: Herding cats

It seems clear Sunflower is not going to budge (their counter-offer was a bit of an insult if anything) and, as such, we unfortunately don't have investor consensus on whether to sell. I had hoped that your finally getting a written offer from Project Sunflower would bring them together, but it was not to be.
The main problem with the three investors is that their funds are at different stages of maturity. So John would be happy to sell now (he hasn't actually come out and said it but I believe he might sell the company for as little as €15 million). At the other extreme is Fashion Equity Partners, who have never had an exit from their new fund (well, not a good one at least) so are pushing for a higher offer. FEP has cash and would prefer to invest more with MissInge and ride the growth curve with you.
Most seriously Tim is saying that he will not agree to any sale at any price without appointing an investment bank and going through an auction process. He says that unless we do that, we can't be sure that we are getting top dollar for the business.
I have a call in to his boss as I think Tim is just passing on the message from his investment committee. Don't hold your breath, though.

Dan Rossi

Chairman
MissInge Fashions

From: Grace Inge
Sent: 29 March 2010 09:43
To: Dan Rossi
Subject: Re: Herding cats

I think we should call the deal off. I have spent the past three months running round the world on Project Sunflower and have neglected the business. The launch in Russia was a flop because I no-showed for the launch so the media think I am anti-Russian. No one wants to be seen in one of our jackets in Moscow. And worst of all, Sunflower knew about the problems before I did.

We will miss the sales target for the quarter as a result and when I tell the Sunflower people, I'm sure their offer will go down or they might even withdraw. So much for "paying a premium price for a strategic acquisition", or whatever it was they said at the time.

I need to get back to running the business – can we call a board meeting and formally pull out of the discussions? How damaging is all this for my relationship with the investors?

I'm feeling a little tender about all this at the moment so looking forward to your advice...

Grace Inge

CEO
MissInge Fashions

From: Dan Rossi
Sent: 29 March 2010 10:50
To: Grace Inge
Subject: Re: Herding cats

It would take two of the three investors to force a sale through, using the drag-along provisions, and there is little chance of that happening at the moment.

Bummer about the quarter's sales – THAT is not going to go down well.

All in all I agree we should withdraw from Sunflower. Next time we go through this we need to be much better prepared and have the investors aligned on process, deal structure and valuation before we engage with a buyer. Having said that, this will be a tough board meeting. Wear some Kevlar!

I will set up a board call for ASAP this week.

Dan Rossi

Chairman
MissInge Fashions

From: Dan Rossi
Sent: 31 March 2010 16:32
To: Grace Inge
Subject: Board feedback

As you know, the board call this morning did not go well. I really must advise you to remain calm whatever happens during board meetings and your heated exchange with Tim was regrettable.

We continued with the meeting after you left and unfortunately some of them are questioning whether you are the right person to lead the company through a sale process. I pressed your case strongly but there is a movement to bring in a "big-hitter" as CEO.

Can we discuss face-to-face ASAP please? And please keep this to yourself for the time being.

Dan Rossi

Chairman
MissInge Fashions

From: Grace Inge
Sent: 2 April 2010 19:29
To: Dan Rossi
Subject: Re: Board feedback

Thanks for the meeting and all the advice over the last couple of days.

When you told me the board wanted to bring in a new CEO my initial reaction was frankly one of relief – I thought it would be great to have someone else take the heat and let me focus on what I enjoy, which is designing and building great products, talking to the press and selling through our various partners.

After we spoke, I now understand that I could not only lose my job but also my investment in MissInge, especially if the new CEO and I don't see eye-to-eye. It hadn't occurred to me that a new CEO would most likely want to raise a new round of investment – he would then have more room for manoeuvre. I also did not see that he would prefer the new investment round to be at a low price – that way his share options are priced reasonably and he can more easily show an increase in company valuation, but I get horribly diluted.

More importantly I have decided that I really don't want to give up at this stage. These past few weeks have been really stressful but I am determined to continue building the company that I founded, so I'm not letting go at this stage.

I hope you agree with my decision, because I value your support and help. My message to the doubters on the board is that the only way I will leave my position is if I am physically dragged away from my desk.

Grace Inge

CEO
MissInge Fashions

From: Dan Rossi
Sent: 7 April 2010 08:17
To: Grace Inge

Subject: Selling the company

Grace,

In your absence this week, I have had a series of one-to-ones with the investors and I am pleased to say there is no longer any talk about replacing you as CEO. I was never really sure how achievable the idea was, even though there was no doubt they were serious at one point. You can thank me for saving your bacon by bringing me back a small jar of caviar from your trip to Russia!

However, they definitely want to start a formal sale process. I know you want to focus on running the business, but if we run a proper company sale process with the right advisers it should be less stressful for you. I can also take some of the heat, if you want.

Good luck in Russia – don't forget to tell them you love them really!

Dan Rossi

Chairman
MissInge Fashions

From: Grace Inge
Sent: 7 April 2010 10:29
To: Dan Rossi

Subject: "From Russia with Love"

Dan,

Sounds good – let's go for it.
Russia might be recoverable BTW; the journalist in question is a bit of a maverick and the shops are still keen to stock the Carrera jacket. Will keep you posted.

Grace Inge

CEO
MissInge Fashions

Chapter 9
Preparing a Company for Sale

> Success depends upon previous preparation, and without such preparation there is sure to be failure.
>
> Confucius

Selling a company should be approached with the same rigour as running any part of a business, in that it requires a process in order to be effective and successful. The process does not necessarily need to be documented or be that formal – it is not a question of ISO9001 certification, for example. But a well-prepared M&A process can help achieve a higher price for the business and increase the likelihood of a transaction going through to completion. Rather like a house that has been on the market too long, a company can get "tired" in the eyes of acquirers if it is marketed for too long. Valuation techniques may be scientific, but possible acquirers also need to be excited about the idea of buying the company – they want to buy something with sizzle.

Selling also takes an enormous amount of valuable CEO time that might be better spent finding new customers and building the company. In some instances it can develop into a full-time job for more than half a year, so it must be very carefully planned.

There are three main phases of the sale of a company:

1. Preparation – get the shareholders aligned on valuation and the founders and key staff to agree on transition, i.e. those who will not stay with the company. Make a considered and formal decision to start the sales process (or not). Have a Plan B – what happens in the event that no one wants to buy the company for a reasonable price (at least discuss the alternatives).
2. Marketing – select advisers, agree terms and brief them. Staff the internal team. Prepare presentation material. Do some pre-due diligence to identify what might increase or reduce the company's value. Prepare the DD data

room. Decide whether to run a formal auction. Contact and engage with potential buyers. Keep the process competitive if at all possible!

3. Transaction – negotiate the term sheet, Sale and Purchase Agreement (SPA) and other legal documents. Perform Due Diligence. Discuss integration and announcement with the buyer.

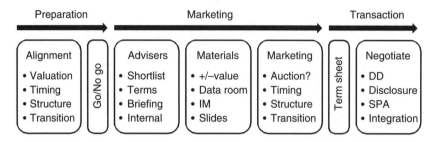

The length of time needed from start to finish varies enormously, but nine to 12 months is typical. The most unpredictable phase time-wise is marketing, where finding one or more interested acquirers can be anything from immediate to very slow.

(It is outside the scope of this book to discuss founder and shareholder agreements, articles of association and so on, but they are important ways of protecting the entrepreneur's and investors' interests when navigating critical milestones in a company's development such as selling the business, or when an expected problem is encountered.)

The place to start: stakeholder alignment

If this step is skipped or glossed over, which it often is, a successful sale of the business becomes much more difficult to achieve. The step is often managed by the investment bank, if one is appointed. In fact it is preferable to run the process before the bank is appointed.

At its simplest, it means agreeing the lowest and target sales price of the business. More completely, it includes understanding the portion of the purchase price that can be at risk, for example through an earn-out and over what timeframe; which of the team remains and who leaves or would prefer to leave; what the financial objectives are for the key players and how the deal would ideally be structured. Is this ideally a sale of the business or its assets? For cash, or would payment in deferred cash, shares or restricted shares be acceptable? Some of these options will be preferred, while others will be an absolute requirement – for example, some VCs cannot or will not accept shares in other companies.

Perhaps most importantly, it includes a Plan B – what happens if the sale of the business does not go through for whatever reason. Does the company stay as it was, or does it seek some other way of providing the shareholders with a liquidity event? This is often a very difficult or inconclusive discussion, not least because some might prefer the Plan B, at a time when everyone needs to focus on Plan A!

In most cases the sale of a business is not an exit – the most commonly used term – because many investors and entrepreneurs will continue to be involved with the acquired company, perhaps because they have agreed to continue working for the new company, or the acquisition has been in shares rather than in cash. Further ties come because of warranties, retained payments and earn-outs. It is better to think of it as a liquidity event, or at least a door to another place rather than an exit to the outside.

Professional investors have different requirements at different times, depending on the state of their fund, their confidence in the company and the management team and the appetite of their LGPs for more investments. They also know that it is very hard to push through a sale against the wishes of the management team.

The first task is to construct an exit spreadsheet. If there have been multiple rounds of finance, this could be quite complicated, especially if there are multiple classes of share, liquidation preferences and dividends. An exit spreadsheet calculates the proceeds and profit for each shareholder at different sale prices. It is based on the calculation of the price per share shown elsewhere, but uses different deal scenario prices to show what each shareholder would get at different prices.

The exit spreadsheet can be used to work out the minimum price that would be acceptable to each group of shareholders. It may be that the options are underwater at a valuation that the investors would be happy to sell, or that an earlier investor would be prepared to sell at a lower price than a later investor. Once you have all the input, you can see whether the price is reasonable in terms of what the company could be sold for. If this is below the level where staff and management receive a return, a carve-out can be negotiated with the investors. This is often difficult but should be done before the sale process is advanced, in that the investors will recognize the need for management to be motivated for the sale of the business to be successful.

A typical carve-out would be constructed along the lines of the first 5 to 10 per cent of the proceeds going to management in the form of a bonus before any payments are made to shareholders. In other words, a carve-out will sit ahead of liquidation preferences and other investor privileges.

Each shareholder and founder should be asked their investment timeframe. VCs' funds have limited lives, so they will perhaps be more open about timing than about valuation, where they will not necessarily want to prejudice a sales process by mandating a valuation.

Finally, some thought should be given to the structure of a deal, or more particularly what aspects of a deal would not be acceptable to an investor. Would they accept shares in the acquiring company in place of cash, for example?

With this, you will have the valuation and timing requirements for each shareholder.

It can be interesting to have preliminary discussions between the entrepreneurs and the investors before the company is ready for sale. The objective of each shareholder in terms of valuation and exit timeframe can be presented as a scatter graph, with one or more dots for each shareholder. It might look something like this:

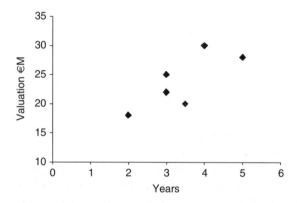

The limits can be boxed, which shows the sweet-spot area of valuation and timing:

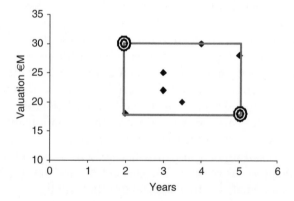

The top-left corner (circled) is a valuation of €30 million in two years and would satisfy everyone. The bottom-right point (also circled) is a valuation of €18 million in five years and would satisfy no one. In between is the area where it should be possible to negotiate a sale to the satisfaction of the shareholders.

Apart from valuations, the stakeholder alignment process should be about transition. Some founders and key staff may wish to leave when the company is bought and others may prefer to stay. It is important to be clear about this to acquirers, because the plans of the key staff may well affect the amount a buyer is prepared to pay for the business. In some cases it may be sensible to agree terms with those who are likely to leave ahead of the process, especially if they are important for a successful sale. CFOs, for example, often lose their jobs when their company is sold but they are likely to be crucial to the success of the transaction.

At the end of this process, the shareholders and board need to make a conscious decision whether to start a sale process. Hold a board meeting, present all the facts and get agreement about valuations, timing, process and key issues.

The process of making a conscious decision also holds true when the company has already been approached by a potential buyer, to decide whether to approach other potential buyers. Sticking with just one buyer is risky, in that there will always be a suspicion that full value has not been extracted. The reverse is also true, in that a buyer will worry about over-paying if there is no competition and will be keen to reduce the price as negotiations advance. Competition can be healthy for both sides.

The best way to achieve a premium valuation and the greatest chance of a sale being successful is to have more than one interested buyer.

Adviser selection

The role of an investment bank in selling a business is similar to that of a real estate agent: it markets the asset through a network of contacts and helps with the negotiation. Banks can also provide an independent valuation, called a fairness opinion, if one is needed.

As with real estate agents, this work can alternatively be done internally by the company. But if a bank is not used, make sure you can reach all possible buyers.

There are two problems and one possible trap with using a bank. First, they are expensive, with typical fees of 3–4 per cent of the transaction and a minimum of perhaps €500,000– €750,000. Secondly, they will not take on all mandates, because their success-fee model requires a high degree of likelihood that the company will actually be sold. You can also end up trapped if the chosen bank is not good enough: most agreements with banks have a "tail" clause, meaning they receive the fee for a period of time after the agreement has been terminated, perhaps 12 months even if they have been fired.

The best way to select an adviser is first to draw up a long-list by asking investors, friends and other contacts for recommendations. Look at their track record and whether they have relevant sector experience. Talk to the principals – this is a relationship business above all and you should feel comfortable that you could work with them. From that, draw up a shortlist of candidates and invite them to present to the board of directors and key shareholders – this is referred to as a beauty parade. Choose the one whose beauty is more than skin-deep.

Most importantly, the banker has to work for the CEO and the company, and not for the investors. Be careful about using an adviser that is recommended by your investors, as the banker has to represent all the various stakeholders.

Follow the same process for the other advisers, especially legal. This is not the time to train your brother-in-law! Choose the best lawyer you can find, who has extensive, relevant (for example cross-border) M&A experience and a great reputation. The right lawyer might not exist in the town where you are based and the expertise may not be present in the company's usual law firm. The lawyer will likely be annoyingly expensive, but as their work can make the difference between personal success and failure, it is very likely to be worth it.

Materials

The two main documents needed are an information memorandum (IM) and a presentation slide deck, which is essentially a subset of the IM. They present the compelling reason why an acquirer should be interested in buying the company. There may also be a "teaser", a summary document without confidential information that can be distributed without an NDA being entered into.

The investment bank helps edit and produce the documents, but, rather than rely on that input, it is best to produce at least the presentation ahead of the appointment of the bank and use it to brief the bank and the other advisers.

As the company progresses, these documents will need to be kept up to date.

Rocks and nuggets

Buyers will base their offer price on the information they receive within the IM and from the presentations. If they are selected, the term sheet will in all likelihood include an exclusivity clause, preventing the seller from looking for better offers while the transaction is being concluded.

Once the term sheet is signed, prices might fall but they almost never increase. Anything discovered that detracts from the value of the company – such as unclean ownership of intellectual property, an off-balance sheet liability such as an upcoming tax charge or a disgruntled key customer may lead to a price reduction. But anything that increases the value – such as unexploited market segments and technology, or a discontinued product that could be resurrected – will not be rewarded with an increase in the price offered, because by then the price is fixed and has been agreed.

These are rocks and nuggets: you stub your toe on both, but only one has value. It is important to identify these hidden issues early on in the process and to share the information with the investment bank.

Bad news will always get out. Good news should be shouted about.

Marketing

This is potentially the most time-consuming and lengthy portion of the process. The CEO in particular will need to make enough time available, while ensuring that the business continues to hit its sales targets (a miss will give the buyer an excuse to reduce the price it is willing to pay for the business).

The bank is responsible for contacting possible buyers, although it is quite normal to find the most interested buyers are in fact already known to the company, such as competitors or companies in adjacent markets.

At the end of this process potential buyers submit offers and the suitor with most attractive offer, normally the highest offer with the greatest likelihood of the deal closing, is invited to exclusive negotiations.

Due diligence

In the same way that the legal term "due process" means following the standard steps in a legal process, due diligence refers to the standard steps taken to ensure all relevant information has been disclosed to a buyer of securities.

It is burdensome, in that the buyer will want to see all legal information about a company, such as customer and supplier contracts and employment agreements, intellectual property rights and any disputes as well as detailed financial information such as budgets and audited accounts, employment agreements and board minutes. This is why the process should be started early, not least to help with the rocks and nuggets exercise.

Before the buyer is chosen, it is sensible to have created a list of documents for due diligence, perhaps in a secure virtual data room which can be accessed by authorized Internet users. That way any missing or unsigned documents can be identified and hopefully dealt with before DD starts in earnest.

Negotiation and closing

In parallel with due diligence, the sale and purchase agreement (SPA) is negotiated, together with any other agreements as needed. The priority in the SPA is risk allocation to protect the buyer from incorrect or incomplete information about the company, and the seller through limitations of liability. The sellers provide warranties (promises) that information is correct and indemnities that financially reward the buyer in the event of financial damage to the company being discovered after it has been sold.

A due diligence document, such as last year's audited accounts, will have a matching warranty in the SPA ("last year's audited accounts are correct") or possibly an indemnity against anything in last year's accounts that turns out to be inaccurate. Just before signing the SPA, the seller will write a disclosure letter to the warranties, identifying and detailing any facts that may not be correct. In this case it might be that there were some non-material errors found in last year's audited accounts, which have been carried through to the current year. Provided a disclosure has been made, the buyer cannot make a later claim for compensation.

This process of due diligence, warranties and indemnities, followed by disclosure is often slow and painful but, done well, will protect the shareholders from later claims by the buyer. Again, the right lawyer can make all the difference in negotiating the best possible outcome and in minimizing the risk.

Professional investors such as VCs do not like giving anything other than basic warranties, such as to confirm they own the shares. So the entrepreneur will almost certainly end up giving more warranties than the investors, and that can justify some financial reward such as a higher share of the escrow account, if there is one.

There may be other ways, depending on the situation, in which an entrepreneur can boost the proceeds from the sale of the company at the time of an exit. First, for a company with a high NFO and a low valuation, reducing the NFO between the time the company is sold and the transaction closes may be a way of getting more cash to shareholders. Secondly, many buyers will want to have some portion as an earn-out, where the amount paid depends on how well the company does in the first year or two under new ownership. VCs generally don't like earn-outs because they have no involvement and no influence during the earn-out period. They have left the board and have little or no management contact. It may be possible to agree a lower but guaranteed amount that goes to the VC, leaving a larger earn-out for the founders and staff.

Integration planning and announcements

There will be a great deal of interest in the transaction, not least from the staff who will want to know what it means for their jobs and career prospects. At the beginning of the sale process, it is important to decide who will know about the transaction (the insiders) and who will not. Typically at least a senior finance person will need to know, and perhaps the head of HR (if there is one). It is important to emphasize the requirement of secrecy. Make sure that the insiders are fully informed about each stage of progress – there is nothing worse than being told that a transaction is imminent but then being kept in the dark! Establish ways of dealing with leaks and rumours – saying that every entrepreneurial company, especially one with venture investors, is always up for sale is not a bad excuse.

As the deal gets close to completion, with its understandable focus on the founders and investors, it is all too easy to forget about option holders, staff, customers, suppliers and the industry in general. An announcement strategy needs to be devised ahead of the actual sale and in cooperation with the acquirer, with a suitable message for each of these groups. Here are a few suggestions:

- Draw up an integration plan together with the acquirer, even if you are not part of the transaction. Help the acquirer understand who the key members of staff are, their strengths and weaknesses. Make sure any reservations you might have about the integration plan are voiced. You are not the decision-maker, but you can play an important role in laying the foundations for successful integration.
- Draw up internal and external communication plans with the acquirer, so that announcements with agreed wording can be made on the respective websites, as well as to customers, industry analysts and suppliers, and staff on both sides.
- As soon as the acquisition is announced, get the acquiring company's CEO or senior management to make a presentation to all your staff, jointly with the company's founders. The presentation should explain why the company has been sold and what the buyer plans to do with the business.
- Arrange a roadshow and series of calls to key customers and business partners so that they can understand what the transaction means for them.
- For every member of staff who has options and/or shares, prepare a simple table explaining how much money they will receive from the sale and when. Show separately any upsides from earn-outs, etc. Be prepared to talk about the tax implications, at least in general terms.
- Encourage the acquirer to consider a retention bonus, such as an additional month's salary for those who are still employed after one year. The acquirer should also make as clear a statement as possible about job cuts, although it does not need to be definitive. "Our priority is growth rather than cost savings" is fine.
- Be clear whether you personally will stay with the acquiring company, or leave. If you want to leave, be upfront with the acquirer and negotiate an amicable termination of your contract of employment as part of the sale. The temptation is to fudge this and to talk about a transition period, along the lines of "I'll be here at least to make sure the integration is a success",

but that may well not work. If you have told the acquirer you are likely to leave after a while, you risk having no authority within that period and of being marginalized. If you are not sure whether to stay and you accept a role within the combined organization, you may disrupt the integration by leaving – it looks like you have tried the combined company and not liked it. If you want to stay for a transition it might be better to terminate your employment contract and work as a consultant for a period of time. The same clarity is necessary for all founders and senior staff – the fact that some are leaving at the time of the sale of the business can give more junior staff greater confidence their own positions are safe, because they are not on the list of people leaving at the time of the acquisition.

- Set up a Q&A, perhaps in the form of an intranet forum. Individuals can then ask questions with the answers visible to everyone. You can pre-populate this with questions you think people might ask, such as what will happen to the brands, whether any products will be discontinued, how the companies will be integrated, whether any offices will be closed or staff relocated, and so on.

Episode 10

The Sale of MissInge Fashions

Money grows on the tree of persistence.

Japanese proverb

The board is gathering together and Grace is feeling a little tense. The atmosphere seems to be as friendly as ever, with smiles and jokes exchanged as coffee is served. They are waiting for Tim before starting the meeting. "Tim is always late," Grace thinks, "and when he's here he spends most of the time on his BlackBerry."

"Good morning, Grace." Dan approaches with a smile. "Ready for the big day?"

"Yes, I think so. Any idea what the reaction is going to be?"

"I haven't spoken directly to any of the board members. I wanted to leave them to think over the information you circulated yesterday. It's great to have a choice, but I think we can be sure it will be a tough conversation. And..."

Grace interrupts. "I know, Dan. I'll be a good girl this time and not be rude to Tim." She smiles at Dan as they share the memory of the earlier board meeting that had nearly led to her being fired. "Where is the charming man, by the way?"

"Just parking, I think. I saw his car from the window a moment ago. We should probably get started with the meeting."

"Please take your seats. Tim will be here in a moment and I want to start as soon as we can. I will see to it that we finish on time." Dan motions to the board table, for everyone to get seated.

The door opens, and Tim enters. "Sorry, guys, bad traffic."

"Hello, Tim, and welcome. We're just starting. Please help yourself to coffee and take a seat." Tim ignores the coffee, takes his BlackBerry from his pocket, sits down and starts to read his email. Grace looks at Dan and slightly raises an eyebrow.

"Right." Dan looks purposeful. "Lady and Gentlemen, thank you for coming to this special board meeting. We only have one item on the agenda, which is to consider the various options to sell the company. Grace? Over to you."

"Thank you, Dan. I hope you have all had the chance to go through the presentation I sent out. I will summarize the options we have and where we are in the M&A process." Grace glances at her notes before continuing.

"You will no doubt remember that the objective was to achieve a higher valuation than Sunflower. To that end we engaged an investment bank to look for alternatives and to solicit offers. They have worked hard and I have presented MissInge to nearly 20 companies that expressed an interest in possibly buying us. That list has been whittled down to just two candidates: Sunflower and the company with the codename Rose. You all know who that refers to."

"Sunflower continues to be interested in us and have actually increased their offer, despite us missing the sales plan last quarter. This is probably because there is competition this time."

"Rose is a listed company, set up and run by a friend of mine – actually we studied together. Rose is listed on the stock market and their interest in us is really about scale; they can't get enough interest from the analysts and brokers at their size. MissInge is smaller in terms of sales, but we have a higher profile in the media and more international sales. Their in-house broker is very enthusiastic about a tie-up with us."

"Rose is offering us 40 per cent of the capital of a combined business. They would issue new shares, so the offer is subject to approval by their shareholders. Their broker thinks getting approval should not be a problem because the existing shareholders really want to get the shares more widely written about, talked about and traded."

"Who would run the company if you merge with Rose?" Tim looks up from his BlackBerry.

"I would. The existing CEO would become Head of Design." Grace can't help looking pleased.

"Are you sure your judgement is not clouded by your career aspirations?" Tim is now very much focusing on the presentation.

"The figures speak for themselves, I think. With Rose, the shareholders get more per share," says Grace.

"Except with Sunflower, we get cash," Tim retorts. "With Rose, we get shares in something that no one is interested in and we lose all our control. So I have no idea how to get the cash back into the fund. Nor at what value; after all, the shares could go up or down. And they'll go down once I start to sell them."

"Tim," Dan interrupts, "we'll have time to discuss the relative merits in due course but please let Grace finish her presentation."

"I just want it clearly understood that I'm very unhappy about this. It should be clear we require cash from the sale of the business. Not bits of paper that I can't sell," replies Tim.

"Hold that for the moment, Tim. Grace, please continue."

"OK, Dan, thanks." Grace takes a breath before continuing with her presentation. "With Rose, both sides are convinced that one plus one will equal three with this combination. We have better design and a stronger brand, while Rose has better logistics and sales channels. They are also better at keeping costs down. We can learn a lot from them. They are really strong in accessories and shoes, both of which fit well with our jackets. There's an integration plan. Their head office is just 5 kilometres from ours and they have enough space to accommodate us – we could give up our office and save the rent. There are many other examples of synergies."

"Their market capitalization is €42 million. They would buy us through an issue of €28 million of shares. The combined market cap would then be €70 million and MissInge shareholders would own 40 per cent. There is no earn-out, no escrow retention and no lock-up period – meaning we get all the shares immediately and we can sell them as soon as we receive them if we wish." Grace is having trouble being neutral, with her clear preference becoming too apparent. She forces herself to calm down and carry on more dispassionately.

"Sunflower has increased its offer, making it more attractive than before. It's now €25 million, €15 million at closing and the remaining €10 million after one year, subject to us hitting our sales targets. They would deduct any warranty claims from the €10 million they are holding back."

"I've prepared a comparison for us to look at, if you could please pass this around." Grace hands round a sheet of paper.

Debt + interest	€ 1,150,000
Liquidation prefs	€ 7,000,000
Accrued dividends	€ 1,500,000
Transaction fees	€ 400,000
Total	~ € 10 million

"In this table, you can see we have about €10 million of overhang, meaning the shareholders get nothing until the debt, liquidation preferences and so on are all paid."

"That means," Grace hands around another piece of paper, "the shareholders receive the following."

	Sunflower	Rose
Proceeds	€15–€25m	€28m
Overhang	€10m	€10m
To shareholders	€5–€15m	€18m

"As you can see, Rose is much more compelling and I would like your approval to go forward in the discussions with them." Grace sits down. If it hadn't been for Tim's earlier outburst, she might have expected a clear green light.

"Thanks, Grace." Dan gestures to the investors around the table. "Comments, questions, views?"

"I can only support Sunflower, as I said earlier," says Tim. "Anything else would be impossible for us to accept. I'm sure that is true for us all." The other investors nod in agreement. "We can't accept shares as payment, especially as they seem nearly impossible to sell. We would own so much of Rose that it would be almost impossible to dispose of our holding. During that time, the share price would be under pressure as the main shareholders all try to sell. It's just unacceptable; Sunflower is the only option."

John, the investor who Grace knows is very keen to sell, leans forward. "Grace, you have done a fantastic job getting these two offers lined up. We all really appreciate and admire the work you have done and it is great to have a choice. But, like Tim, I really can't accept illiquid shares. I don't think you would find any professional investor who would. Did you ask Rose for a cash alternative?"

"Yes, John, we discussed it at length. Rose does not think it would be possible to raise the cash in the current environment," Grace explains.

"Well, that's further evidence that we're right," answers John. "If Rose can't sell their own shares for cash, how could we?"

"Let's stop the conversation there," suggests Dan. "We all need time to think over the issues. Perhaps the investors could think about a carve-out for management? Grace, perhaps you could discuss with Rose again the question of a cash offer?"

"Unless anyone has any other comments, let's close the meeting and I will arrange a follow-up in the next very few days. Could you please each call me to discuss the issues?"

Everyone nods in agreement and without much more than farewells being said, the meeting ends.

From: Grace Inge
Sent: 12 July 2010 11:12
To: Dan Rossi

Subject: Rose

Hi Dan,

I've bottomed out the issue of a cash offer with Rose over the past several days and it really is not going to happen. It seems no one is prepared to buy shares at the current price – their broker even told me (after a couple of glasses of wine!) that they were surprised how well the share price had held up over the past few weeks.

I think it is looking too risky to go forward with Rose – I will now focus on Sunflower, discreetly while we wait for the investors' decision on a carve-out! By the way, the latest from Sunflower is that they are starting to think this is more strategic than a bolt-on acquisition. I've been asked if I want to move to California! That would be cool!

Thanks for the help. Sunflower will work if I can get the investors to share the spoils with the staff somehow. I'm pleased I won't be in on your meeting – Tim in particular is behaving as if I just sold his mother into slavery.

Good luck!
Grace Inge
CEO
MissInge Fashions

Dan's mobile rings.

"Dan Rossi speaking."

"Hi, Dan, this is Tim. I promised to come back to you about MissInge Fashion's various options. Is this a good time?"

"Yes, Tim, it is. And thanks for calling back. Have you been able to reach a decision with the other investors; one that you are all happy with?"

"Maybe, but I'm personally not at all happy. It seemed to me the last board meeting was staged to put pressure on the investors to agree a carve-out. The whole Rose idea is a non-starter, but it enables Grace to take the moral high-ground about how Sunflower isn't paying enough, and that all the money is going to the investors. Remember we've stuck it out with this investment through good times and bad. And now I'm expected to give away part of my investment. I've thought for some time that she's out of control. I still think we should have brought in someone with some more experience."

"Hang on, Tim. She's built this company herself to where it is. She's one of the most written about, talked about and admired young business leaders in the country today. She alone is responsible for the sales growth, for making the company attractive for someone to buy. She's got two real offers, even if you don't like one of them. With either option, your fund will make money. I think you're being a little harsh."

"I wanted you to know I'm not happy."

"Message received, Tim. Do you have a solution?"

"I've spoken to the other investors and we're prepared to offer the management a carve-out of 10 per cent of the proceeds from Sunflower in addition to anything the shares might be worth. That means the founders and option holders receive another €1.5 to €2.5 million, making it comparable to the paper offer from Rose. But a condition is that we go exclusive with Sunflower, as soon as possible. No more messing about."

Dan decided not to rise to the bait of the "paper offer" and the "messing about".

"That's great news, Tim, and I'm sure it will help Grace be more receptive to the Sunflower offer. In my experience, we haven't quite seen the end of the negotiations – it wouldn't surprise me if we see her able to improve the offer further. You might not like it, but she has become a financially aware, mature business woman over the past year. And she's now a great negotiator."

Tim grunts in grudging acknowledgement.

Sunnyvale, California. September 1, 2010

IF acquires MissInge Fashions

IF International Fashions has concluded its acquisition of privately held MissInge Fashions, a European-based company with a leading position in designing high-quality apparel, especially jackets.

In addition to an initial consideration of 15 million euros (about 20 million dollars), there are earn-out fees of up to 10 million euros (about 13 million dollars) and a retention bonus for key staff of 3 million dollars. Grace Inge, MissInge's founder and CEO, will join IF as Executive Vice President, Branded Products, reporting directly to the CEO. The sales, manufacturing and logistics functions will be immediately integrated into IF's global network but the distinctive brand MissInge will be retained.

A spokesman for IF said, "The MissInge acquisition enhances IF's existing quality branded apparel products, one of IF's fastest growing and most profitable market segments. We are excited about leveraging the MissInge brand into other product areas, with its must-have appeal to young affluent buyers. This will be spearheaded by Grace Inge, who is joining IF in a senior executive role. She is moving to California to assume her new role."

Grace Inge said, "I am really excited to be starting my new role in as great a company as IF. MissInge has lots of growth ahead of it and I am really pleased that I can continue to play a key part in its further development. I am looking forward to moving to California."

The acquisition is slightly dilutive to IF's current year's earnings, but is expected to be accretive from next year onwards.

<u>About IF</u>: IF International Fashions is one of the fastest growing fashion conglomerates with the vision to have a strong presence across all the main fashion segments, on a global basis. By combining an extremely responsive and efficient supply chain with focused brand development and a global footprint, it maintains a cost and brand advantage over its competitors.

Chapter 10
The Lessons of MissInge Fashions

"Begin at the beginning," the King said gravely, "and go on till you come to the end: then stop."

Lewis Carroll

We started out by saying there are four things every entrepreneur needs to know about finance. This is a brief summary of what, if you forget everything else, are the main learning points.

1. Operating cash

- Measuring and optimizing cash is not just for manufacturing companies, it applies to media, software and service companies too.
- Sales growth requires funding, and faster growth requires more funding.
- The amount of funding needed and when it is needed can be calculated.
- Operating cash requirements should be built in to the product management process.
- Regularly review and if necessary change the way the company works with its suppliers, customers and internally, especially when an invoice is raised rather than the days of credit granted.
- Sort customers and products by the amount of operating cash they require and focus on the best ones.

2. Raising investment

- The four items that affect the economic value to the entrepreneur are the pre-money valuation, liquidation preferences, accrued dividends and anti-dilution. Consider all of these when negotiating the right deal, not just the valuation.
- A high valuation with full ratchet anti-dilution is a toxic combination.

- The investor's financial objectives, such as a minimum absolute return or a multiple, may distort the valuation of the business.
- Carry out some due diligence on the VC: find out the age of the fund that is investing and talk to another investee company.
- Get into the detail and negotiate hard – the points are more negotiable than most think.
- Construct an exit cap table and attach it to the term sheet or investment agreement.
- Use the best possible lawyer with relevant experience, who may not be local or known to you.

3. Staff equity

- Most staff do not understand equity and options.
- Issuing options is better for the company than shares, not least because they can be cancelled when an employee leaves.
- Have the right to buy back shares from a departing staff member or partner, and exercise it.
- Set the option exercise price as low as possible, remembering that the ordinary shares are worth less than investor shares.
- Get good tax advice.

4. Selling the company

- Make a conscious decision with all the main shareholders before starting the process.
- Construct a best guess exit spreadsheet on the assumption the transaction is cash and debt free. Keep it up to date during the sale process.
- Align everyone on valuation minimums and expectations.
- Select and appoint your own adviser, not necessarily the one recommended by the investors.
- Agree or at least think about a Plan B if the sale is not successful.
- Agree transition plans for the key team members – who will not stay with the acquisition?
- Running a sale process is very time-consuming, make sure the company's operations do not suffer. Missing the sales target during a sale process will reduce the price for the business.
- Be open with a potential buyer about all the bad and all the good points of the business.
- Do some integration and internal announcement planning before the deal closes.
- Use the best possible lawyer with relevant experience.

A closing thought

A company's key drivers are likely to consist of very few numbers or Key Performance Indicators (KPIs). For some companies, sales orders, EBITDA and NFO might be enough. Combining a few numbers, a little understanding and a healthy dose of common sense is a powerful way of analysing and managing a company financially. We are not great fans of ratios, as it is generally better to look at the real numbers or to graph the trends. For example, a company with no surplus cash and a low NFO would have very low or negative current and quick ratios. The conventional view on ratios is that such a company lacks cash. We disagree and would view it as a great achievement!

We wish you the very best of luck in making money for you and your shareholders.

Appendix 1

MissInge's P&L and Balance Sheet

These numbers are downloadable as a spreadsheet from http://www.palgrave.com/products/title.aspx?PID=411830 perhaps?

Base numbers

Missinge Fashions

P&L in €000			Recent Years			Forecast			
			2007	2008	2009	2010	2011	2012	2013
Sales		(1)	180	1,350	2,592	10,653	16,022	19,373	23,248
Raw material Microfibre			−65	−473	−855	−3,409	−4,807	−5,812	−6,974
Raw material others			−41	−305	−570	−2,301	−3,365	−4,068	−4,882
Manufacturing			−27	−203	−311	−1,087	−1,634	−1,976	−2,371
shipping (percentage of sales)	2.8%		−5	−38	−73	−298	−449	−542	−651
Gross margin			42	332	783	3,558	5,768	6,974	8,369
Personnel costs		(2)	−280	−560	−2,170	−2,520	−3,080	−3,430	−4,130
Operating costs as % of Headcount	40%	(3)	−112	−224	−868	−1,008	−1,232	−1,372	−1,652
EBITDA			−350	−452	−2,255	30	1,456	2,172	2,587
Depreciation	25%	(4)	0	−5	−34	−518	−963	−957	−865
EBIT			−350	−457	−2,289	−488	493	1,215	1,723
Financial expenses net	13%	(5)	0	0	0	0	−460	−664	−677
EBT			−350	−457	−2,289	−488	33	551	1,045
GM			23%	25%	30%	33%	36%	36%	36%

Drivers			2007	2008	2009	2010	2011	2012	2013
Sales growth	*(%)*			650%	92%	311%	50%	21%	20%
Seasonality	*(%)*	(1)							
Raw Material:									
Microfibre as % sales	*(%)*		36%	35%	33%	32%	30%	30%	30%
Raw Material: other as									
% sales	*(%)*		23%	23%	22%	22%	21%	21%	21%
Manufacturing as %									
sales	*(%)*		15%	15%	12%	10%	10%	10%	10%
Headcount of an									
average cost of	*70 €*	(2)	4	8	31	36	44	49	59
Capex in €	*(Euro)*		20	120	1,970	2,300	940	586	678
Accounts receivable	*(days)*		60	60	60	60	60	60	60
Days of Raw Material									
Microfibre	*(days)*		33	33	33	33	33	33	33
Days of inventory									
finished goods	*(days)*		75	75	75	75	75	75	75
Account payables									
Microfibre	*(days)*		0	0	0	0	0	0	0

Notes

(1) the quarters have been calculated with the same seasonality each year

(2) the personnel costs are assumed to be as shown per head in Europe. The personal costs in China are part of the COGS

(3) Operating expenses are calculated as a percentage of the EU Headcount

(4) Deprecation is calculated as a %age of the previous year's fixed assets (this is a simplification as it does not include depreciation of this year's Capex).

(5) Financial expenses are calculated on the credit of the previous period.

(6) Cash is surplus cash. The company does not need cash for running its daily business.

(7) The days of raw material for both (Microfibre and other) are 15 days

(8) The days of WIP are 45 days, based on daily raw material and half manufacturing

(9) MissInge pays suppliers other than Microfibre in 30 days

(10) Accruals are calculated as a percentage of monthly personnel costs.

(11) The government loan is a 7 year bullet loan with accrued interest.

			Recent Years			Forecast			
Balance (€000)			2007	2008	2009	2010	2011	2012	2013
Cash		(6)	421	1,927	1,405	0	0	0	0
Inventories			40	297	532	2,095	3,017	3,648	4,377
Raw Material		(7)	8	56	102	408	581	702	843
Work in Progress	12d	(8)	4	29	53	208	300	362	435
Finished Goods			29	212	377	1,478	2,136	2,583	3,100
Receivables			30	225	432	1,776	2,670	3,229	3,875
Current Assets			491	2,450	2,368	3,870	5,687	6,877	8,252
Fixed Assets			20	135	2,071	3,853	3,830	3,459	3,272
TOTAL ASSETS			511	2,585	4,440	7,724	9,517	10,335	11,524

Continued

Continued

Balance (€000)			Recent Years			Forecast			
			2007	2008	2009	2010	2011	2012	2013
Credit			0	0	0	3,537	5,105	5,210	5,165
Trade payables		(9)	3	25	48	192	280	339	407
Accruals	35%	(10)	8	16	63	74	90	100	120
Current liabilities			12	42	111	3,802	5,475	5,649	5,693
Government soft loan	7.5%	(11)	500	1,000	1,075	1,156	1,242	1,335	1,436
Share capital (Founders + Angel)			350	350	350	350	350	350	350
Share capital investors			0	2,000	6,000	6,000	6,000	6,000	6,000
Equity			0	1,543	3,254	2,766	2,799	3,350	4,396
TOTAL LIABILITIES AND EQUITY			511	2,585	4,440	7,724	9,517	10,335	11,524

Balance (€000)	Recent Years			Forecast			
	2007	2008	2009	2010	2011	2012	2013
NFO	59	481	853	3,605	5,317	6,437	7,725
Fixed assets	20	135	2,071	3,853	3,830	3,459	3,272
Net assets	79	616	2,924	7,459	9,147	9,896	10,997
Long Term Debt	500	1,000	1,075	1,156	1,242	1,335	1,436
Equity	0	1,543	3,254	2,766	2,799	3,350	4,396
Financing	500	2,543	4,329	3,922	4,041	4,686	5,831
Cash surplus (+), Credit (–)	421	1,927	1,405	–3,537	–5,105	–5,210	–5,165
Cash generated per year	421	1,506	–523	–4,941	–1,568	–105	45

Operational Finance	Recent Years			Forecast			
	2007	2008	2009	2010	2011	2012	2013
NFO	59	481	853	3,605	5,317	6,437	7,725
WC	480	2,408	2,258	68	212	1,227	2,559
Cash surplus (+), Credit (–)	421	1,927	1,405	–3,537	–5,105	–5,210	–5,165

Scenario – growth of 75 per cent p.a. from 2011

P&L in €000		Recent Years			Forecast			
		2007	2008	2009	2010	2011	2012	2013
Sales	(1)	180	1,350	2,592	10,653	18,643	32,625	57,094
Raw material								
Microfibre		–65	–473	–855	–3,409	–5,593	–9,788	–17,128
Raw material others		–41	–305	–570	–2,301	–3,915	–6,851	–11,990
Manufacturing		–27	–203	–311	–1,087	–1,902	–3,328	–5,824
shipping								
(percentage of sales) 2.8%		–5	–38	–73	–298	–522	–914	–1,599
Gross margin		42	332	783	3,558	6,711	11,745	20,554
Personnel costs	(2)	–280	–560	–2,170	–2,520	–3,584	–5,776	–10,143
Operating costs as								
% of Headcount 40%	(3)	–112	–224	–868	–1,008	–1,434	–2,311	–4,057
EBITDA		–350	–452	–2,255	30	1,694	3,658	6,354
Depreciation 25%	(4)	0	–5	–34	–518	–963	–1,072	–1,416
EBIT		–350	–457	–2,289	–488	731	2,586	4,938
Financial expenses								
net 13%	(5)	0	0	0	0	–460	–805	–1,346
EBT		–350	–457	–2,289	–488	271	1,781	3,593

Balance (000€)	Recent Years			Forecast			
	2007	2008	2009	2010	2011	2012	2013
NFO	59	481	853	3,605	6,187	10,841	18,971
Fixed assets	20	135	2,071	3,853	4,288	5,663	8,529
Net assets	79	616	2,924	7,459	10,475	16,504	27,500
Long Term Debt	500	1,000	1,075	1,156	1,242	1,335	1,436
Equity	0	1,543	3,254	2,766	3,037	4,818	8,411
Financing	500	2,543	4,329	3,922	4,279	6,153	9,846
Cash surplus (+), Credit (–)	421	1,927	1,405	–3,537	–6,195	–10,351	–17,654
Cash generated per year	421	1,506	-523	–4,941	–2,659	–4,155	–7,303

Scenario – NFO improved to 9 per cent

P&L in €000			Recent Years			Forecast			
			2007	2008	2009	2010	2011	2012	2013
Sales		(1)	180	1,350	2,592	10,653	16,022	19,373	23,248
Raw material Microfibre			−65	−473	−855	−3,409	−4,807	−5,812	−6,974
Raw material others			−41	−305	−570	−2,301	−3,365	−4,068	−4,882
Manufacturing			−27	−203	−311	−1,087	−1,634	−1,976	−2,371
shipping (percentage of sales)	2.8%		−5	−38	−73	−298	−449	−542	−651
Gross margin			42	332	783	3,558	5,768	6,974	8,369
Personnel costs		(2)	−280	−560	−2,170	−2,520	−3,080	−3,430	−4,130
Operating costs as % of Headcount	40%	(3)	−112	−224	−868	−1,008	−1,232	−1,372	−1,652
EBITDA			−350	−452	−2,255	30	1,456	2,172	2,587
Depreciation	25%	(4)	0	−5	−34	−518	−963	−957	−865
EBIT			−350	−457	−2,289	−488	493	1,215	1,723
Financial expenses net	13%	(5)	0	0	0	0	−119	−116	0
EBT			−350	−457	−2,289	−488	374	1,099	1,723

Drivers			Recent Years			Hypothesis			
			2007	2008	2009	2010	2011	2012	2013
Growth of sales	*(%)*			650%	92%	311%	50%	21%	20%
Seasonality	*(%)*	(1)							
Raw Material:									
Microfibre as % sales	*(%)*		36%	35%	33%	32%	30%	30%	30%
Raw Material: other as % sales	*(%)*		23%	23%	22%	22%	21%	21%	21%
Manufacturing as % sales	*(%)*		15%	15%	12%	10%	10%	10%	10%
Headcount of an average cost of	*70 €*	(2)	4	8	31	36	44	49	59
Capex in €	*(Euro)*		20	120	1,970	2,300	940	586	678
Accounts receivable	*(days)*		60	60	60	2	2	2	2
Days of Raw Material Microfibre	*(days)*		33	33	33	7	7	7	7
Days of inventory finished goods	*(days)*		75	75	75	56	56	56	56
Account payables Microfibre	*(days)*		0	0	0	30	30	30	30

Balance (000€)			Recent Years			Forecast			
			2007	2008	2009	2010	2011	2012	2013
Cash		(6)	421	1,927	1,405	0	0	358	2,016
Inventories			40	297	532	1,474	2,128	2,574	3,088
Raw Material		(7)	8	56	102	162	234	283	339
Work in Progress	12	(8)	4	29	53	208	300	362	435
Finished Goods			29	212	377	1,104	1,595	1,929	2,314
Receivables			30	225	432	59	89	108	129
Current Assets			491	2,450	2,368	1,533	2,217	3,039	5,233
Fixed Assets			20	135	2,071	3,853	3,830	3,459	3,272
TOTAL ASSETS			511	2,585	4,440	5,387	6,047	6,497	8,505
Credit			0	0	0	916	894	0	0
Trade payables		(9)	3	25	48	476	681	823	988
Accruals	35%	(10)	8	16	63	74	90	100	120
Current liabilities			12	42	111	1,465	1,665	923	1,108
Government soft loan	7.5%	(11)	500	1,000	1,075	1,156	1,242	1,335	1,436
Share capital (Founders + Angel)			350	350	350	350	350	350	350
Share capital investors			0	2,000	6,000	6,000	6,000	6,000	6,000
Equity			0	1,543	3,254	2,766	3,140	4,239	5,961
TOTAL LIABILITIES AND EQUITY			511	2,585	4,440	5,387	6,047	6,497	8,505

Balance (000€)	Recent Years			Forecast			
	2007	2008	2009	2010	2011	2012	2013
NFO	59	481	853	984	1,447	1,758	2,109
Fixed assets	20	135	2,071	3,853	3,830	3,459	3,272
Net assets – to be financed	79	616	2,924	4,838	5,276	5,216	5,381
Long Term Debt	500	1,000	1,075	1,156	1,242	1,335	1,436
Equity	0	1,543	3,254	2,766	3,140	4,239	5,961
Liabilities & equity – financing	500	2,543	4,329	3,922	4,382	5,574	7,397
Cash surplus (+), Credit (–)	421	1,927	1,405	–916	–894	358	2,016
Cash generated per year	421	1,506	–523	–2,320	22	1,252	1,658

Operational Finance	Recent Years			Forecast			
	2007	2008	2009	2010	2011	2012	2013
NFO	59	481	853	984	1,447	1,758	2,109
WC	480	2,408	2,258	68	552	2,115	4,125
Cash surplus (+), Credit (–)	421	1,927	1,405	–916	–894	358	2,016

Capitalization table

Invested €000		2007	2008	2009	2010
Grace Inge		50	50	50	50
Dan Rossi		300	300	300	300
Investors		0	2,000	6,000	7,000
Total invested €000		350	2,350	6,350	7,350
Ownership %		**2007**	**2008**	**2009**	**2010**
Grace Inge		60%	34%	25%	15%
Dan Rossi		40%	23%	17%	10%
Investors		0%	29%	43%	60%
Employee option pool			15%	15%	15%
Post-money valuation €000		750	7,000	27,094	6,000
Pre-money valuation €000		450	5,000	23,094	5,000
Accrued Dividends		**2007**	**2008**	**2009**	**2010**
Annual cost €000	10%	0	200	600	700
Cumulated €000		0	200	800	1,500

Exit Model

Exit Valuations €000		€ 15,000	€ 20,000	€ 25,000
Liquidation Prefs	1x	–7,000	–7,000	–7,000
Debt		–1,156	–1,156	–1,156
Accrued Dividends		–1,500	–1,500	–1,500
To shareholders		5,344	10,344	15,344
Grace Inge	15%	802	1,552	2,302
Dan Rossi	10%	534	1,034	1,534
Employee option pool	15%	802	1,552	2,302
Investors	60%	3,207	6,207	9,207
Investors Total		11,707	14,707	17,707
Grace Inge		5%	8%	9%
Investors Total in %		78%	74%	71%

Appendix 2
Survey Results

> I have made this letter longer than usual,
> only because I have not had the time to make it shorter.
>
> Blaise Pascal

Survey background

In September and October 2009 a survey was carried out of as many European Venture Capital firms as possible in cooperation with IESE, the business school in Barcelona.

A total of 421 VC firms were identified and contacted throughout Europe; 110 answers were received, of which 84 were complete.

The purpose of the survey was to explore the relationship between entrepreneurs and VC firms from a valuation and term sheet perspective, in particular:

- Identify which valuation techniques are most commonly used, and understand whether these depend on the country, stage of investment or industry.
- Understand which terms are universal in that they appear in all or nearly all term sheets, and those that appear only occasionally.
- For the terms that affect the economics of the investment, identify their frequency of use and how negotiable they are in the overall investment mix.

The questionnaire contained 37 questions, divided into three sections:

- Demographics
- Term sheets
- Valuation.

Demographics

Survey results were received from 17 European countries, led by the two largest markets for Venture Capital, Germany and the UK:

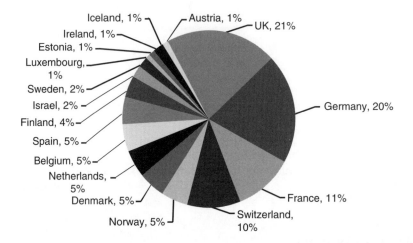

The survey was sent to senior staff and 78 per cent of the respondents held executive positions:

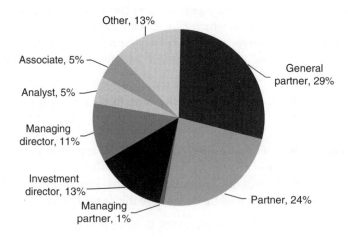

They invest across the main growth areas, including software, biotech and clean tech:

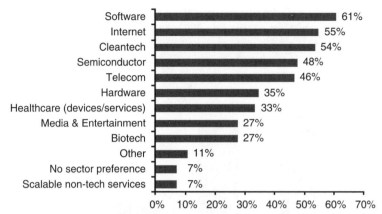

The investment stage focus was mostly on early stage companies, but not seed rounds. Each stage can be defined as:

- Seed – the business exists as a concept but the company has no product (it might have something to show but it is not a commercial version) and no paying customers.
- Start-up – the company and product exist and the first customers are trialling the product or service. There may be a launch customer and some revenue.
- Growth – the company has customers and products and is looking for funds to expand, often in sales and marketing.
- Expansion – the company is well established with measurable market share, brand and product recognition. It may be profitable. The funds raised are to help expansion, often to set up international operations or to make acquisitions.
- Transfer – the company is well established and looking to sell or to IPO. The funding is intended to strengthen the company's balance sheet and may not be essential to the company's survival.

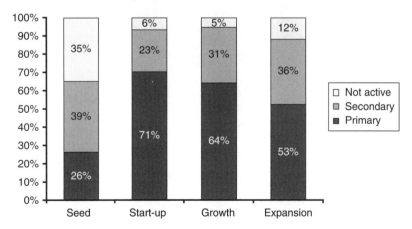

Although most VCs prefer to invest in their own country, most will invest in other countries, especially within Europe:

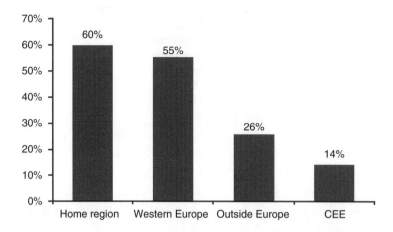

The largest group has less than €100 million of funds under management:

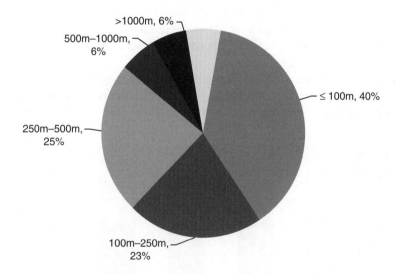

The average number of portfolio companies is 29:

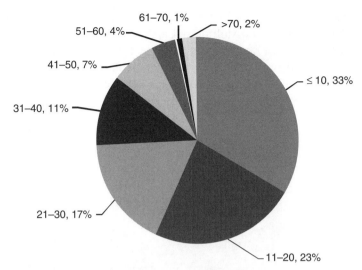

The most recently raised fund was quite small, perhaps reflecting the economic situation at the time of the survey:

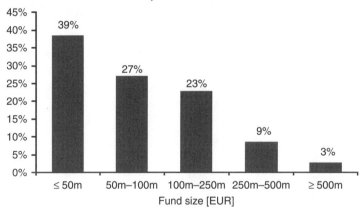

The preferred investment size for an "A" round investment is €1 to 2 million:

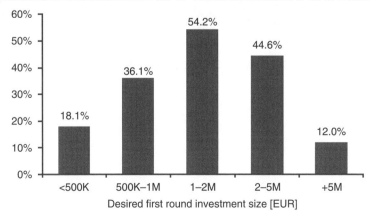

The majority of firms use both main investment target methods – IRR (Internal Rate of Return) and Multiple of Capital (the main difference is that IRR is an annual percentage rate whereas Multiple of Capital is an absolute value, independent of the length of time of the investment. It is calculated by dividing the money the investors receive by the money invested – cash over cash):

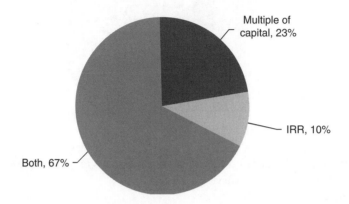

Much has been written about the relatively poor returns from venture capital, especially in Europe. The survey supported this view, with 35 per cent achieving an IRR of less than 10 per cent. (It is also worth noting that many refused to answer, with only 26 replies to this question.)

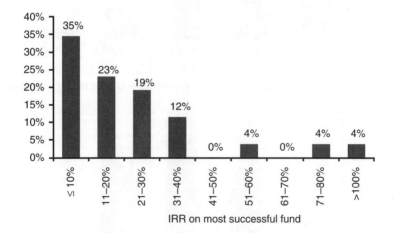

The majority achieved a 2x to 3x multiple of capital on the most successful fund:

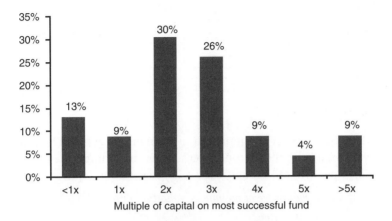

With about half the VC firms targeting a 3x multiple:

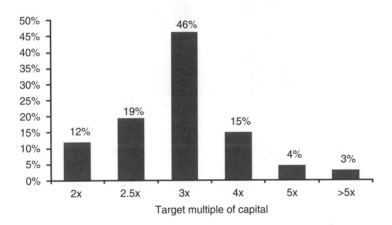

Term sheets

In this section, the survey asked how often particular terms are used in term sheets, and how often each becomes a key negotiation topic. As an example, this is an extract from the survey, with the possible answers being "always/ often", "sometimes" or "rarely/never":

	Frequency of Usage	Crucial Negotiation Topic
Pre-Money Valuation	☐	☐
Employee Option Pool	☐	☐
Key Man Insurance	☐	☐
VC Expense Reimbursement (due diligence costs, etc.)	☐	☐
Representations/Warranties	☐	☐
Confidentially	☐	☐
Exclusivity & Target Closing Date	☐	☐

Pre-money valuation

Unsurprisingly, the most common and most highly negotiated item was pre-money valuation, with 99 per cent of term sheets including a pre-money valuation and 94 per cent of the time it was a key negotiation topic:

Q: "Please describe your usage of pre-money valuation in the INITIAL term sheet."

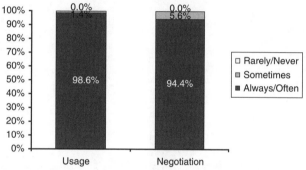

Accrued dividends

Dividends are less common, with 63 per cent sometimes or always seeking rights to dividends. Note how rarely this key issue is discussed – only 12 per cent of the time is it a key issue and over half the time it is just accepted by the entrepreneur. First the initial position of the investor:

Q: "Please describe your usage of Accrued Dividends in the INITIAL term sheet."

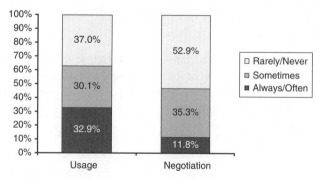

After negotiations, the final usage of dividend accruals is reduced, but still common in about half of executed term sheets:

Q: "In FINALIZED/EXECUTED term sheets how often do you use a dividend accrual clause?"

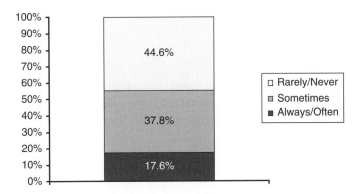

Liquidation preferences

Liquidation preferences are always included in nearly 80 per cent of initial term sheets, 98 per cent always or sometimes. They are also a hot negotiation topic:

Q: "Please describe your usage of Liquidation Preferences in the INITIAL term sheet."

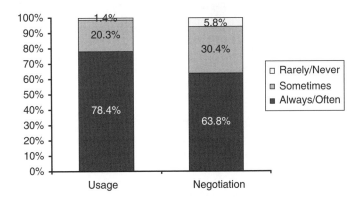

Investors were also asked how negotiable multiple liquidation preferences are:

---

18. When you use a Liquidation preference what multiple do you most often propose at the beginning of a negotiation and where does that number usually settle in the finalized term sheet? (e.g. 2x settling at 1x in final)

Original Proposal ☐

Final proposal ☐

The response showed that while liquidation preferences are commonly used, they are relatively negotiable, with 30 per cent asking for multiples of 2x or above but only 11 per cent executed at that level. Some 65 per cent get executed at 1x preference:

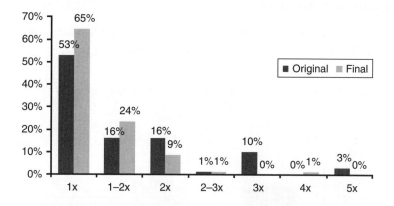

Investors were also asked to what extent they are prepared to give up the participation or double dip right in liquidation preferences. Again this showed their willingness to negotiate the term, although nearly half won't or are unlikely to change:

Q: *"When you use a participating Liquidation Preference (Double-Dip), how willing are you to change to non-participating wording instead?"*

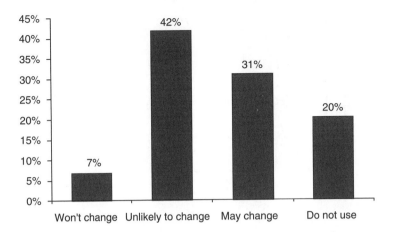

Founders shares

In order to protect their investment from founders leaving, VCs sometimes require entrepreneurs to convert their shares into a new class that vest back to the entrepreneur over a number of years. This effectively means the entrepreneur loses ownership then earns it back. The argument is that founders should be discouraged from leaving a venture that has recently been funded. The use of founders shares is less common in later stage investments, where the entrepreneurs have already "earned" their share ownership over many years.

Q: "Please describe your usage of Founders Shares in the INITIAL term sheet."

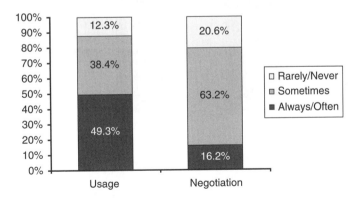

There may also be restrictions placed on the transfer or sale of Founders Shares during the vesting period.

Q: "Please describe your usage of Restrictions on Transfers of Founders Shares in the INITIAL term sheet."

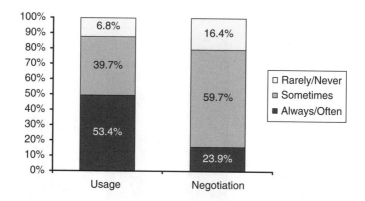

Anti-dilution

Anti-dilution terms enable investors to receive additional shares in the event that future rounds of investment are at a lower price, a sort of price protection for their investment. The clause is very common, being present in 95 per cent of term sheets, but despite their potentially toxic nature, they are only hotly negotiated in 39 per cent of cases.

Q: "Please describe your usage of Anti-Dilution in the INITIAL term sheet."

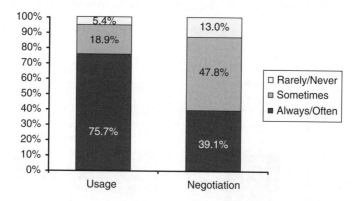

The trick with anti-dilution terms is to understand how they would work and to focus on reducing the damage anti-dilution could cause. One way is to use a weighted average between the higher and lower share prices and to limit the anti-dilution in time. Entrepreneurs are natural optimists and often struggle with the idea that future investment might be at a lower price. Negotiating anti-dilution can be thought of as an insurance policy – no one wants to think the worst will happen but it is best to be well prepared! Negotiating the anti-dilution clause is especially important for entrepreneurs who focus on achieving a high pre-money valuation only to find a later investment round is at a lower price.

Investors were also asked what method of anti-dilution was finally agreed. The most aggressive form – full ratchet protection – is always or often present in about a third of term sheets.

Q: "In FINALIZED/EXECUTED term sheets how often do you use the following methods of anti-dilution?"

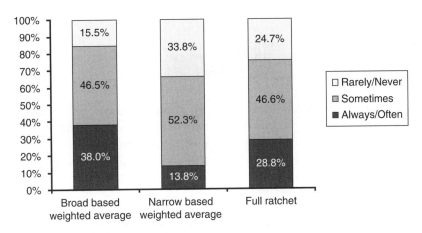

Redemption rights

A redemption clause gives the VC the right to force the entrepreneur to provide an exit, for example by finding a replacement investor. The clause itself is by no means universal, and it is often not a hot negotiation topic:

Q: "Please describe your usage of a Redemption Right in the INITIAL term sheet."

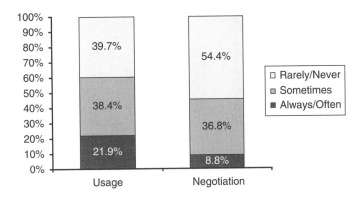

Q: *"In FINALIZED/EXECUTED term sheets how often do you use a Redemption term?"*

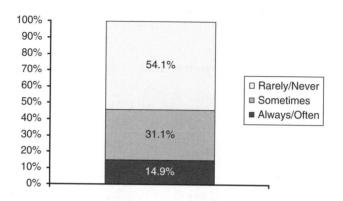

In fact it is an important clause, worthy of more thought and negotiation effort than it usually gets. As it is not a very common term, it may be possible to negotiate its deletion, or to water it down by for example enabling redemption in steps (e.g. one-third at a time). Also, penalties that give the investor an extra return on redemption need close scrutiny by the entrepreneur and justification from the investor.

Redemption can be in the form of the initial investment plus some kind of premium, or the market value of the investment at the time of redemption. Investors were asked what form they most commonly used:

Q: *"In a Redemption Clause, which of the following pricing structures is most frequently used?"*

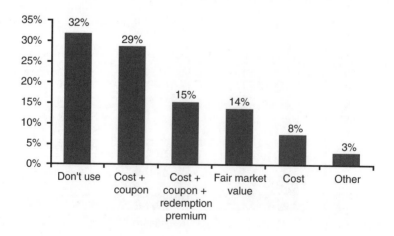

Tag-along, drag-along rights

These provisions give investors the right to sell shares on the same terms when other shareholders sell part of their shares (tag-along) or to force other investors to sell when they sell their shares (drag-along). Both terms are quite common and probably impossible to remove. Negotiation focuses on the detail of how the terms work, the thresholds and any exemptions that do not trigger the tag-along, drag-along rights.

Q: *"Please describe your usage of Tag-Along in the INITIAL term sheet."*

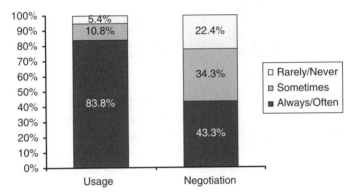

Q: *"Please describe your usage of Drag-Along in the INITIAL term sheet."*

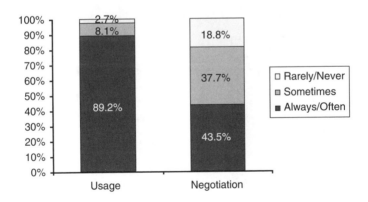

Right of first refusal/pre-emption provisions

A right of first refusal (RoFR) term gives the VC the right to buy more shares, should any other shareholder wish to sell, and is a common term. Negotiations focus on how it will work, such as exclusions for tax planning.

Q: "Please describe your usage of a Right of First Refusal in the INITIAL term sheet."

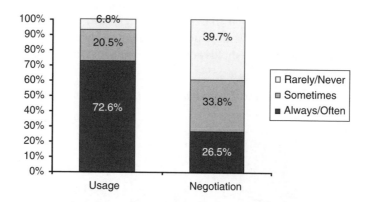

Pre-emption provisions work in the same way as RoFR, but for new share issues. Similarly, negotiations focus on how the provisions work rather than whether the term is present in the agreement. It may make sense, for example, to limit pre-emption rights to shareholders with a minimum number of shares in cases where there are a large number of shareholders and the process of offering small numbers of shares around might be burdensome.

Q: "Please describe your usage of a Pre-emption Right in the INITIAL term sheet."

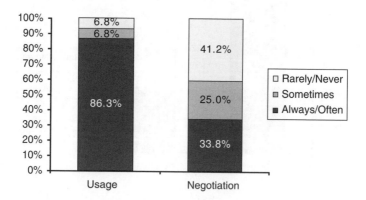

Employee option pool

Allowing management to create an option pool and to grant options to employees is a common term:

Q: *"Please describe your usage of an Employee Option Pool in the INITIAL term sheet."*

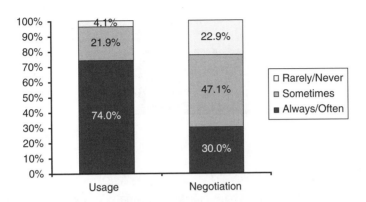

Investors were also asked about the size of the option pool:

Q: *"What is the typical post-money percentage allocated to the Employee Option Pool in your primary investment stage?"*

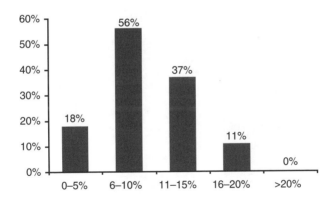

This result would probably look different with US ventures where option pools of 15 per cent or more appear to be more common.

Investors were also asked about their willingness to top up the option pool during future rounds. Without a top-up, employees would quickly lose their percentage stake in the business:

Q: *"Do you top up/add to the Employee Option Pool with future rounds of investment?"*

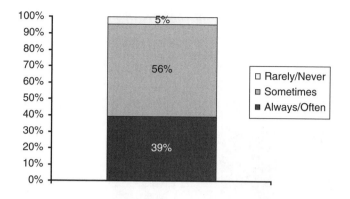

IPO clauses

Term sheets may define what happens if the company is floated on a stock market, as an Initial Public Offering (IPO). The VC may seek Registration Rights, meaning that they get the right to manage the IPO if the company goes public. These clauses become more relevant the later the stage of the company.

Q: "Please describe your usage of Registration Rights in the INITIAL term sheet."

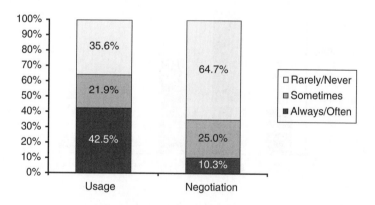

There may be also a requirement on the founder not to sell at the time of the IPO, called a lock-up.

Q: "Please describe your usage of Post-IPO Management Lock-Up in the INITIAL term sheet."

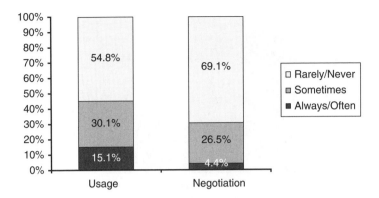

Management Information Rights

This term gives the VC a legal right to regular information about the company, especially its financial performance. It is a common term and should not be contentious.

Q: "Please describe your usage of Management Information Rights in the INITIAL term sheet."

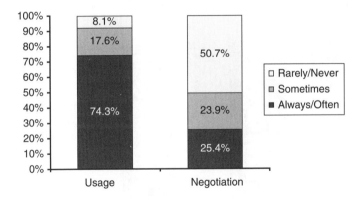

Board representation and other board rights

This term gives the VC the right to observe board meetings, or to have one or more seats on the board. Sometimes it includes the ability to appoint more directors under certain circumstances, to ensure that the VC can vote through actions as it wishes. So it may need careful negotiation, even if the term itself is common.

Q: "Please describe your usage of Board Representation Rights in the INITIAL term sheet."

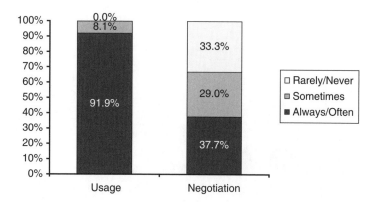

Investor consents

This term defines what management is not allowed to do without board and or investor approval. It often includes corporate structural and financial issues such as granting options, paying dividends and setting up new companies. It might include budget restraints such as buying assets above a certain value or hiring highly paid staff. The term is common, but the detail needs to be carefully thought through and negotiated.

Q: "Please describe your usage of Investor Consents/ Shareholder Vetoes in the INITIAL term sheet."

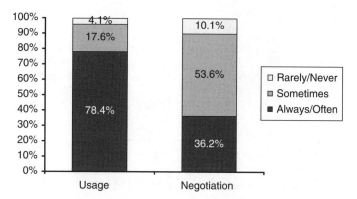

Voting rights

This term defines what voting rights the investor has, which may be more (or sometimes less) than the actual shareholding held by the VC. The desire to have more votes gives the VC better control over the company. A lower voting right may be to avoid falling foul of local takeover legislation. It is a common term, with negotiation focusing on giving as little additional voting away as possible, rather than removing the right.

Q: "Please describe your usage of Voting Rights in the INITIAL term sheet."

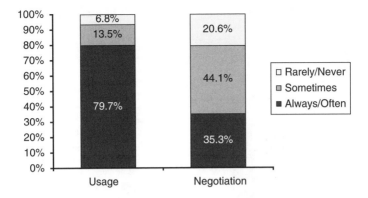

Material adverse change

This enables an investor to change his mind if the company has not performed as planned – the business has changed materially. An example of its use is when the investment is being made in tranches. By only calling down monies from their LPs when they are absolutely needed, the IRR of the fund can be optimized. It is not that common a term and needs very careful negotiation to prevent it being used by the VC just as a way of changing his mind about the investment.

Q: "Please describe your usage of Material Adverse Change in the INITIAL term sheet."

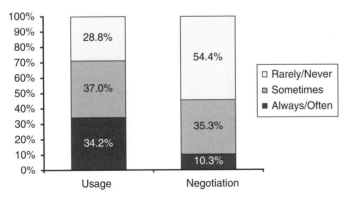

Restrictive covenants/management non-compete

VCs will want to prevent founders and key management from, for example, leaving the company and setting up another company in competition. The idea is quite reasonable!

Q: "Please describe your usage of Restrictive Covenants in the INITIAL term sheet."

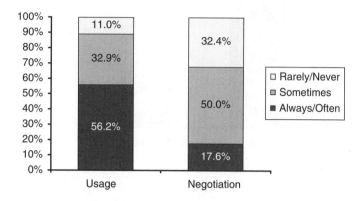

Management employment agreements

Investors may want to make sure they are comfortable with the terms of the founders' employment, including rights to bonuses and termination notice. This term makes entering into employment agreements a Closing Condition of the investment. Although by no means universal, this term requires careful negotiation and, where there is more than one founder or employee concerned, that each is aware of the term and prepared for the negotiation.

Q: "Please describe your usage of Management Employment Agreements in the INITIAL term sheet."

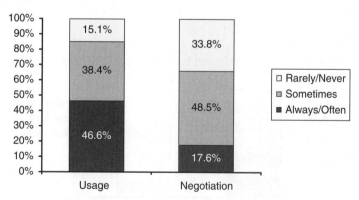

Good leaver, bad leaver

This clause defines what happens to the shares of departing employees (options are generally set up to expire when employees leave), with good leavers perhaps allowed to keep their shares while bad leavers are forced to return them. A good leaver might be someone who is made redundant, becomes incapacitated or dies (the thought that dying makes you a good leaver is perhaps a little macabre). A bad leaver might be defined as someone who resigns or is dismissed for a reason other than redundancy.

Q: "Please describe your usage of good/bad leaver in the INITIAL term sheet."

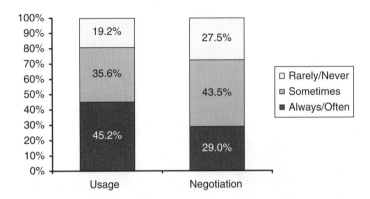

Keyman insurance

Also referred to as key person insurance, keyman compensates the company with a fixed amount of money for possible financial losses as a result of the death (or sometimes incapacity) of certain "key" members of the team. Investors take the view that in the early stages of a company's development, its success depends on certain individuals. A keyman insurance policy protects their investment, so many investors insist on the investee company taking out a policy. It is not a contentious term.

Q: "Please describe your usage of Keyman Insurance in the INITIAL term sheet."

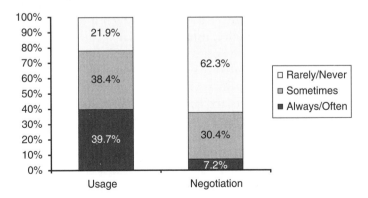

VC expense reimbursement

Most venture firms manage other people's money, the limited partners of the VC fund. So investors avoid incurring costs that will just come out of their management fee and will seek to have their legal costs and perhaps other expenses paid for by the investee company (for the same reason, VC will generally not provide bank guarantees). This is generally neither particularly contentious nor negotiable, other than perhaps to achieve a cap on expenses.

Q: "Please describe your usage of VC expense reimbursement in the INITIAL term sheet."

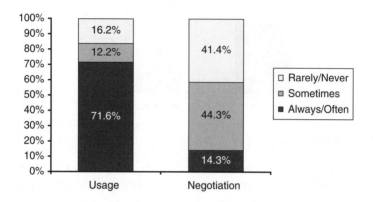

Representations and warranties

As part of the investment process, the entrepreneur will provide a lot of information about the company, the market and the product or service the company is producing or contemplating producing. In order to separate out which of these are opinions and which are facts, investors ask for a representation, which is essentially a promise, or a warranty, which is a promise backed by some kind of financial guarantee, usually personal.

Reps and warranties can be positive (e.g. that the sales pipeline has a certain minimum value) or negative (e.g. that the company is not being accused of breaching another company's intellectual property). Their presence is pretty standard in term sheets and they cannot normally be negotiated away. Negotiations will focus on a time limit for claims and perhaps a cap in total value.

This can be an extremely disturbing term for the entrepreneur as he is being asked to provide a personal financial guarantee. The VC's argument is that it concentrates the entrepreneur's mind to ensure the information which the VC has relied on to make the investment decision is complete and accurate.

Claims against entrepreneurs for breaches of reps and warranties are thankfully rare.

Q: *"Please describe your usage of Representations and Warranties in the INITIAL term sheet."*

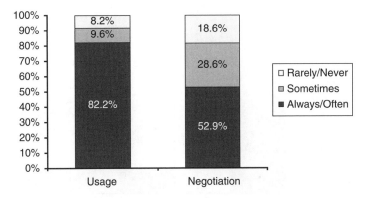

Confidentiality

Maintaining confidentiality of aspects of the investment and the information provided to the investor is a common term, with negotiations focusing on the scope and perhaps the duration of the confidentiality obligation.

Q: *"Please describe your usage of confidentiality in the INITIAL term sheet."*

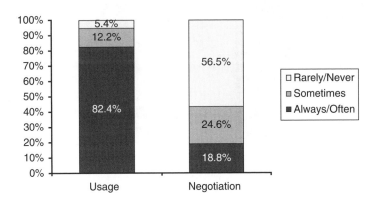

Exclusivity, target closing date and closing conditions

Once the entrepreneur has negotiated and signed the term sheet, the VC will look to be able to complete the investment without the risk of being displaced by another investor. So term sheets might contain an exclusivity term and a target closing date, as well as closing conditions that might be for example that a keyman insurance policy is in place. Again, the presence of these terms is not particularly contentious; it is more a question of agreeing the detail.

Q: "Please describe your usage of Exclusivity and Target Closing Date in the INITIAL term sheet."

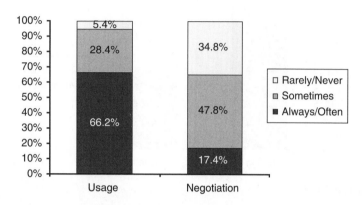

Q: "Please describe your usage of Closing Conditions in the INITIAL term sheet."

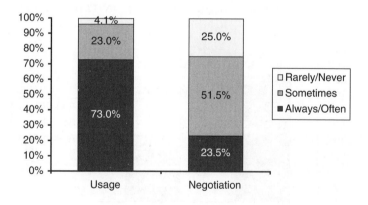

Valuations

Most investors look to invest for five years, at the end of which they need a liquidity event or some other way of realizing an exit from their investment.

Q: "What exit time horizon do you consider most often on your initial investment? (Please specify all that apply.)"

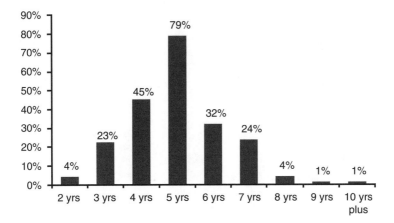

Four main valuation techniques were identified:

- Discounted Cash Flow (DCF), calculating the present value from the cash generated by estimating the sale price and the exit date of the company (e.g. what is the present value of the company if it's worth €20 million in three years' time, which is likely to be a good time to sell the business).
- Exit multiple, which looks to achieve a multiple of the amount of money invested, ignoring the length of time an investment is held, by estimating the sale value of the company in the future (e.g. VC wants a 10x return on the money invested).
- Sales/earnings multiples, which estimates the present value of the company but ignores the future value (e.g. the company is worth 2x times last year's revenues).
- Minimum return, where (e.g. VC wants a minimum €2 million from each investment).

For companies at each stage of development, investors were asked which technique they used and what rates they applied. Many investors use more than one technique.

Q: "Do you use a Discounted Cash Flow approach when valuing companies in the following stages?"

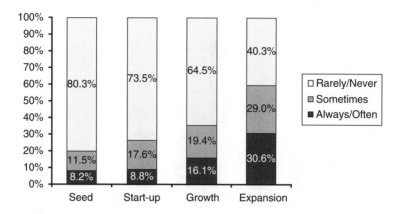

DCF is more commonly used as companies mature, because the cash flows, the timing of an exit and the value achieved become easier to estimate and predict.

Q: "If yes, what annual discount rate do you usually apply (in %)?"

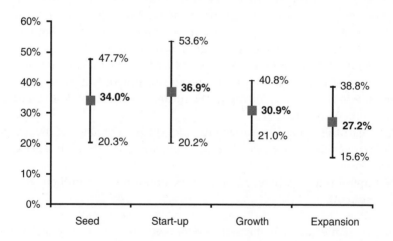

The discount rate used is a combination of the cost of the money and the risk of the investment. As companies become established, risk reduces and the rate used declines. The lower discount rate for seed investments is a surprise, perhaps due to the relatively small sample size, being the stage when fewest investors are active.

Q: "Do you use an Exit Multiple when valuing companies in the following stages?"

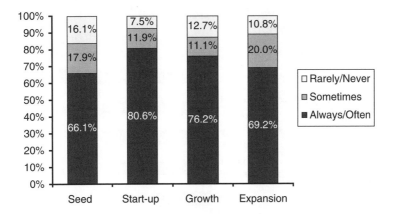

Exit multiples are commonly used in all stages and, as one might expect, the size of the exit multiple is higher the earlier the stage of the business:

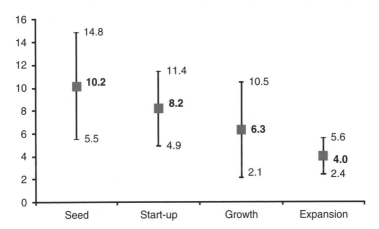

(The bars represent the mean and one standard deviation.) The results mean that, for example, on average a VC is looking for a return of €10.20 for each €1 invested in a seed round investment.

The VCs were asked how exit multiples were calculated – did they just make an educated guess based on their own experience, rely on management projections in the business plan, or look at similar businesses where the value could be calculated (for example they had been sold or were listed on a stock market)?

Q: *"How do you estimate the FUTURE value (exit value) of early stage businesses? (Please choose all that apply.)"*

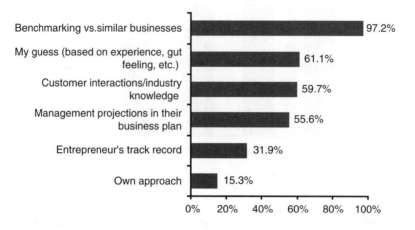

Q: *"Do you use sales or earnings multiples when estimating the PRESENT value of a company (not the future value) (e.g. we value this company at 2x its current sales)?"*

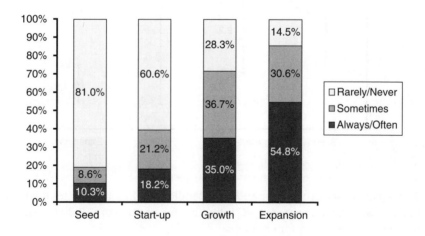

As the company develops, revenues and profits become more significant and measurable, so become more important as valuation metrics.

Q: *"If yes, what multiples do you use? (Please choose all that apply.)"*

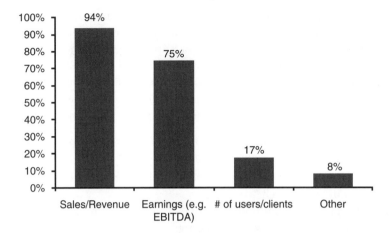

Revenues are the most important multiple, probably because many early stage businesses are not yet profitable. And bubble-era metrics such as users or eye-balls are out of fashion.

Q: "Do you require a minimum euro return on exit (e.g. I want to make at least €2 million on my investment)?"

Only 23 per cent of investors polled seek an absolute monetary return, with 77 per cent saying they do not.

Investors were also asked whether they used Monte Carlo simulations, a technique that is used when there are a large number of inputs, each with a significant uncertainty. A Monte Carlo simulation examines each item that could affect the valuation such as the size of the market, the market share achieved, profitability, even macro-economic trends. The probability of each scenario is estimated and an investment simulation combines the scenarios by running multiple calculations, often several thousand. The results enable statistical significance to be calculated along the lines of "There is a 90 per cent chance of an outcome equal to or better than ..."

Q: "Do you use Monte Carlo simulations when valuing early stage companies?"

Only 1 per cent of respondents always or often use Monte Carlo simulations, with 7 per cent using them sometimes and 91 per cent rarely or never using them. This probably reflects the difficulty of estimating scenarios accurately with early stage companies.

Follow on investments

Venture investments are often made in multiple rounds, typically called seed, then "A", "B", "C" and so on. This potentially makes valuation calculations hard, as the number of rounds and their size are normally not known or esti-mated by entrepreneurs. Rounds of investment may be to achieve a particular milestone (e.g. producing a working prototype, or getting the first customer) and how much investment is needed afterwards may be hard to estimate.

The following are some of the most pertinent replies to the question about investment rounds. The obvious conclusion to be drawn is that there is no sin-gle scientific method for taking all rounds of finance into consideration:

Q: "Could you please briefly describe how you take into account possible future rounds of finance when conducting company valuations?"

"Ballpark – each round will cause 30 per cent dilution. Likelihood that prefer-ences will build up in each."

"We estimate a second round pre-money value and then estimate how much we invest. This gets our new shareholding."

"Applying judgement/sensitivity to financial forecasts and applying past experience of the type of business being evaluated and the typical funding amounts such a business may require to an exit."

"Backward approach, simplified: take exit value, divide by [FD post/total investment amount plus reasonable buffer round]."

"When investing in a company, we assume no further rounds. When the need for new financing arises, this will be treated as a new investment."

"Using probability trees to estimate additional funding required – from us and overall – and effects on shareholding, exit valuation, returns."

"We try to imagine how many following rounds will take place and suppose that the valuation will increase by 50 per cent between each round."

"Should be confident of achieving milestones so next round is an up round. So we should price this round accordingly so next round won't be a down round. Want to own at least 15 per cent on exit, after taking new rounds into account."

"In current environment, ensure that all the financing needs are met by the current syndicate – i.e. no new investors required."

"We always take in account a three-rounds lifetime before exiting. First round accounts for 25–30 per cent of our planned investment."

"Always assume additional rounds of financing at flat valuations, i.e. no change in share price, with outsider-led financing, pro-rata insider participa-tion, option pool top-up and resulting dilution of shareholding."

"Always estimate how much money is necessary to reach maturity/exit and then decide how to allocate the investment over the different rounds."

"We almost always take into account possible future rounds. We size our initial investment so that we have reserves for future investments. The earliest stage, the lowest multiple on liquidation preferences. Ratchet and anti-dilution provisions in case of future down round."

In summary, early stage valuation is about rules of thumb and based more on experience than anything else. As companies develop, the techniques become more sophisticated.

Country differences

The survey results did not differ materially between Germany and the United Kingdom, the two largest countries in the survey, nor could differences be found with other countries. It may well be that results from US investors would be different, but it would appear that European VCs structure and negotiate their investments in a fairly homogenous way.

Appendix 3
P&L and Balance Sheet – An Accounting View

Not everything that can be counted counts,
and not everything that counts can be counted.

Albert Einstein

A very successful entrepreneur, who has founded and run many companies, recently said that his accounting training had been "three hours long, and it was all I needed". We are going to do better: by the end of reading this appendix, which should take a lot less than three hours, you should know all the basics of company accounts. It may take years for an accountant to be trained in all the aspects, but we don't need to go that deep.

As individuals, we think of our personal finances in terms of cash. We have cash in our bank accounts and wallets. We owe a certain amount to the credit card company and the mortgage provider. We don't generally adjust our financial situation if we haven't yet received the electricity bill, or if we've already paid for the flights to visit the parents next Christmas. What we're saving at the moment is simply the salary we've received, less what we've spent. We can measure our savings and loans by looking at the statements from the different providers.

This is called cash accounting, and it works well for individuals and for charities. Very small companies and sole traders are often allowed to use cash accounting because it is easy to manage and calculate. That can mean some advantages, for example not having to pay VAT to the tax authorities until you have been paid by your customer. Cash accounting is simple and intuitive but company value creation is not the same as having lots of cash.

For most companies, cash accounting is not considered accurate enough to measure financial performance and instead use accrual accounting, the idea that costs are incurred at a different time to payment being made. A mobile phone company offering a prepay telephone service does not make more profit than one which bills its customers at the end of each month just because it collects cash ahead of providing the service. Company A, which pays its suppliers on time, is not less profitable than identical Company B that pays suppliers consistently late.

Profitability comes from the business of making and selling products and services, not when the cash changes hands. So the first objective in company accounting is to measure the profitability of the actual business, not merely the ins and outs of its cash flow.

A furniture builder is also not necessarily less profitable if it buys a new machine to turn wood rather than hire the equipment as its competitor does. In fact the former might well be more profitable, even though at some point in time it has less cash, because buying in the long term might be cheaper than hiring. So the second objective is to provide a system that measures the costs of investing in equipment, buildings and even in other companies, separately from the profits from operating the business.

The third objective is to separate company performance from investment such as share capital, which increases when shareholders invest cash in the company. Profits have not been made (in fact it may have some costs in connection with the investment to account for), even though cash has increased. Capital can of course go both ways, and dividend payments to shareholders also need to be kept separate from profits.

So the main elements of company accounts were born: the Profit and Loss account, which measures profitability but ignores cash and the Balance Sheet, which lists the company's assets and liabilities.

Looking at both the P&L and the Balance Sheet, you can analyse a company's performance. There are other reports produced, such as Sources and Uses of funds or Cash Flow Statement, but almost everything you need to know about a company can be found in the Balance Sheet and in the P&L.

The problem is that company accounts are just reports: they represent the financial position of the company at any one time. They don't tell you how to run the company better. They are tools to help us understand a business, to answer the key questions about evaluating a new business:

- Does the business make sense? Does it have a sound business model, is the model working or likely to work, and is the company operationally sound? This is the role of the P&L, and why it is broken down into the different steps to measure profitability, the three main ones being the Gross Margin, which measures the amount of value the company is adding; Operating Profit or EBITDA, whether the company is being run efficiently, and Net Profit to measure whether the company can achieve a return for shareholders.
- What does the company have and need, in terms of equipment and production (the assets) in order to operate? How well is the company financed – is

it financially sound (the liabilities)? This is where the balance sheet comes in. A good way to think of a balance sheet is as a photograph. It is a snapshot of all the company's assets and liabilities. Balance sheets will say the date of the snapshot, such as "... as of 31 December 2009". The P&L shows what happens over time, along the lines of "...for the 6 months ended 31 December 2009". To understand how things have changed since the last accounts date, you will need to look at the previous balance sheet too. The problem with photographs is that the moment they capture might not be representative and that is true of balance sheets too. It is often the difference between two or more balance sheets that is more interesting than the value of items in a single balance sheet.

The P&L

The Profit and Loss account (also called the Income Statement, especially in the US) is the company's scorecard. If the balance sheet is a photograph, the P&L is a movie camera, filming a company's performance over time. It measures financial performance from trading over a period such as a year. It starts with the sales value, or revenue (hence the expression the "top line"). It then follows the simple equation in five or six discrete steps:

sales − expenses = profit

The steps are separated to show how the profit can be explained by its different drivers.

This is the structure of a P&L:

Revenue	
Cost of goods sold	_____
Gross profit	
Operating expenses	_____
EBITDA	
Depreciation, amortization	_____
EBIT	
Interest charges	_____
PBT	
Taxes	_____
Net profit	_____

Step one: product profitability

This calculates the gross profit (or margin) of the business. "Sales" can also be called "turnover" (especially in Germany and the UK) or "revenue" (US). We will use the word "revenue". The formula is:

revenue – cost of goods sold = gross profit, or more commonly gross margin

"Cost of sales" (also called "cost of goods sold, or COGS") is the cost of producing or buying in the items that are sold, excluding taxes such as VAT. It is the cost of product manufacture for a manufacturer, or the cost of service for a service company, or the cost of the item that is being resold for a reseller. It includes the labour cost of the sales, so for example a consultancy company will show the costs of its consultants' time in COGS.

The gross profit is also called a company's "value-add". If a framing company buys glass and wood for €3 to make frames with €2 of labour that it then sells for €15, it has added €10 of value.

It's worth making the point here that investors are interested in high-margin businesses, because it implies lots of differentiated value is being created. Generally high value-add business are harder to compete with and more likely to prosper in the long term. So gross profits are often expressed as a percentage, calculated by dividing the gross profit by the revenue. You might hear a manufacturing company say "We have 60 per cent margins", which just means that for every €10 of sales, the company spends an average of €4 buying in and manufacturing whatever it is they sell. As Mark Spade wrote in his delightful business book from 60 years ago called *How to Run a Bassoon Factory*: "There are two main sorts of business: (1) Buying something and making something out of it. This is called manufacturing. (2) Buying something and making a lot out of it. This is called retailing." What he was doing was measuring gross profit.

Some companies, such as software firms, have very high gross margins because it costs little or nothing to produce another copy of the software to sell. COGS does not include the cost of developing the software, just the cost of making another copy. This might be the cost of the printed user manual or a CD but this is less likely these days, with digital downloads. If any royalties need to be paid to third parties for the software product, they would be counted as COGS. COGS can also include sales commissions (but not sales salaries), and customer support costs.

Step two: operating profit

This takes the gross profit and subtracts the running costs of the business, like this:

gross profit – overheads = operating profit

The overheads are typically shown in one of two forms: people costs (salary, pension, social security etc), office (buildings, telecoms) and other (advertising, PR, trade shows, travel, etc.), or by department: research and development (all the costs of that department), sales and marketing (the people and activities of those departments and general and administrative (meaning the administration of the company). Both ways are interesting, and which you choose depends on what you are interested in monitoring.

Operating profit – there is no difference between the words "earnings2" and "profits2" – is also called EBITDA (Earnings before Interest, Taxes, Depreciation and Amortization). Interest and taxes are not operational expenses, but why are depreciation and amortization removed? If a start-up is amortizing the costs of a company purchase, a license or perhaps the costs of development an ASIC, it can distort the operating performance of the company. The costs being depreciated or amortized have almost certainly already been paid for, so EBITDA is closer to a measurement of cash (although it is not the same, not least because it does not reflect fluctuations in cash needed for operations, the NFO). There is not unanimous support for EBITDA as a profit measure, as its nickname "earnings before I tricked the damn auditor" implies. But it is a good measure of operational efficiency.

Step three: non-financial profit

Earnings Before Interest and Taxes (EBIT) is the profit after accounting for the depreciation of assets and the amortization of goodwill from acquisitions. It is the total profit excluding the financial and tax costs of the business.

EBITDA – depreciation & amortization = EBIT

Step four: pre-tax profit

From EBIT, the financing costs of the business are removed, to measure the costs of banking and other loans:

EBIT – interest = PBT (profit before tax)

Interest costs are measured separately because financial costs do not help us understand operational profitability. Consider two identical companies, one funded by bank debt and other by investor equity; the debt-funded one would produce less net profit, even though the gross margins and operating profits are the same, because interest costs are not deducted and dividends are not.

Step five: after-tax net profit

Taxes are now deducted to show the net profit:

PBT − taxes = net profit

This is also where tax credits and other government incentives for small companies are included. It is unusual in small companies for this step to be positive because of credits or tax refunds, making the Net Profit higher than the pre-tax profit.

Step six: exceptional costs

Exceptional costs include restructuring, write-offs and discontinued operations. As their name implies, they are of a one-off nature and so shown separately, if at all.

Here are the steps in summary:

1. Gross Margin measures product profitability. This is the revenue from the sale minus the cost of the product or service. The GM is the value that is added by the business.
2. EBITDA – Earnings before Interest, Taxes, Depreciation and Amortization. This is the Gross Profit minus the costs and overheads of running the business, or the company's operational efficiency.
3. EBIT – Earnings before Interest and Taxes – the profit after accounting for the depreciation of assets and the amortization of goodwill from acquisitions. It takes into account the investments the company has made.
4. PBT – Profit before Taxes – the profit after the interest charges for any company debt, the costs of the financing the company.
5. Net Profit or Profit after Taxes – after corporation taxes have been accounted for; the profit that is left for the shareholders.
6. Exceptional Items. Not always present, it measures the profit after exceptional or one-off costs that are not part of the company's normal business.

What to look for in a P&L

- The revenue size and growth help to understand the size and growth of the potential market: is this an attractive market to have a business? How fast is the company growing? With P&L reports covering several periods, you can also see whether the growth is consistent and if quarterly or monthly figures are available, spot any seasonal effects, such as Christmas. Does the revenue vary, perhaps because of infrequent large orders? Lumpiness increases the risk to a company's financial health.
- The gross margin is important in understanding the value their customers place on the offering. It is interesting to look at gross margin development

over time, to see whether there are any price or cost trends. How do the gross margins compare with similar companies, are they higher or lower, and why? Gross margin is a measure of the attractiveness of the business model, and investors prefer higher gross margin businesses. In earlier stages of development, it may be that gross margin will be lower, as it is more expensive to manufacture or businesses are just less efficient when they start up. Gross Margin also answers the question of business viability – does it or how quickly is it expected to cover the overheads? Gross margin is not a perfect proxy for business model attractiveness, but it is a great start.

- EBITDA is the measure of the operational efficiency of the company. If gross margin tells us the attractiveness of the business model, EBITDA tells us how well the company ran that business model. Many start-ups are unprofitable, but that does not mean they are badly run, just that the level of sales is still low. The company is not yet mature in its development and is investing in the future to grow the business. But over time, you would expect the operating costs to rise less quickly than the gross margin, leading to profit. EBITDA is increasingly becoming the preferred KPI of profitability for two important reasons, control and cash. EBITDA covers items that are under management control (sales, manufacturing costs, overhead expenses) and not those that are outside their control (depreciation, taxation, finance costs). It is also the closest link to cash, in that the company's operational cash flow is:

Operational cash flow = EBITDA + NFO changes

The operational cash flow can be used to buy more fixed assets, pay finance charges or taxes, or to pay dividends to shareholders.

The P&L only tells you whether the business is capable of generating a profit for its shareholders; it is not trying to do anything else. To understand a company, you need to look at the balance sheet too.

Balance sheet

If a P&L tells you whether a company is economically sound, a balance sheet tells you whether a company is financially sound. It shows which items need financing and how they are financed.

A balance sheet always balances because it is based on the simple formula:

what you have = what you own – what you owe

Let's express this in a personal context. Suppose the only thing of value you own is an apartment worth €300,000. On that property, there is a mortgage of

€200,000. Assuming you own nothing else, and do not owe any money, your net worth is €100,000 according to the formula above. When you started, you might already have had the €100,000, or perhaps when you bought the apartment, it was only worth €200,000. It doesn't change the formula either way.

In a balance sheet, items you own are called "assets", what you owe are called "liabilities" and what you have is called "equity". So the formula then becomes:

equity = assets − liabilities

With a bit of basic algebra, we can change the formula to:

assets = liabilities + equity

Assets are on the "left" of the balance sheet, and the liabilities and equity on the "right".

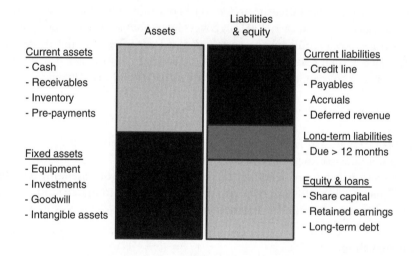

Assets consist of everything the company owns, from cash to buildings. Buildings, equipment and shareholdings in other companies do not change much and might be difficult to sell in a hurry, so they are called "fixed assets". Other assets that are more liquid, called "current assets", include cash, accounts receivable (meaning invoices that have not yet been paid by customers), inventory (items that are held before being sold to customers) and pre-payments. Pre-payments may for example be rent that has to be paid in advance.

Liabilities consist of the company's debts, including bank overdraft or loans, accounts payable (invoices from suppliers that have not yet been paid) and expenses that have been accrued. An example of such an accrual is payroll taxes, which are often not paid until the month after they are deducted from salaries. In other words, the company has cash that belongs to the government, and to correctly represent that in the balance sheet, that amount is listed as a liability. As with assets, liabilities are either current (such as bank overdraft and payables), or long-term (such as a debt that does not need to be repaid for a few years).

Balance sheets are sometimes shown in other ways. Increasingly they are "upside down", with fixed assets at the top and cash at the bottom but otherwise they are the same. In some countries current liabilities are subtracted from current assets rather than being shown on the other side of the balance sheet. Although companies in different countries may show balance sheets with different layouts, words or levels of detail, the basic principles of balance sheets are the same the world over.

Notice that some items might appear on either side of the balance sheet, the obvious one being cash, which can appear either as an asset or a liability, depending on whether there is surplus cash or a credit line.

Pre-payments and accrued liabilities are similar, in that they are both business expenses that have either been paid early or the invoice has not yet been received. Accrued liabilities often exceed pre-payments, because of the deferred nature of taxation.

Cash includes all the cash balances in the various bank accounts or elsewhere such as in the petty cash box. Foreign currency is converted at the rate of exchange of the date of the balance sheet. Short-term investments (those that can be readily converted into cash) are included. They are often shown as "cash equivalents", "short-term investments" or "marketable securities", but in effect they are as good as cash. Cash that is blocked, for example because it is needed for a bank guarantee, and is not available for use by the business is shown as restricted cash. Let's look at the example of Google's balance sheet from 31 December 2009, which shows cash and cash equivalents of $10,198 million (i.e. $10 billion) and $14,287 million of marketable securities.

So on 31 December 2009, Google had $10,198,000,000 + $14,287,000,000 = $24,485,000,000 in cash. Its cash balances increased by about $8.6 billion during 2009, as seen by comparing the cash figures with the previous year. Where did that extra cash come from? By examining the P&L and balance sheets, we can work out that about $6.5 billion came from profits, $2.8 billion from improvements in NFO and the balance from various investment activities.

Receivables, also called "accounts receivable" or in the UK "debtors" (people who are in your debt), is the sum of all the invoices that you have raised that have not yet been paid, including the balances of those that have not been paid in full. Invoices in foreign exchange are converted at the rate of the day of the balance sheet. Invoices that are about to be raised, or work that has been done but not yet invoiced are not included here, but shown as Work in Progress, or WIP. Often, invoices that are not expected to be paid because the customer cannot or is refusing to pay are reduced by making a "provision" against them. These provisions for so called "bad or doubtful debts" may be shown separately. Finally, invoices that are not due for payment within the next 12 months may also be shown separately. For example, a single invoice may be raised for the two-year maintenance of equipment. If half is payable now and half in two years' time, the second half will appear separately as "Amounts due in more than 12 months".

From the 2009 Annual Report of Daimler AG, the car company, it reported €5,675 million of trade receivables, less €390 million of doubtful accounts, giving a net carrying amount of €5,285 million. Of these, €8 million mature after more than one year.

This means that, on 31 December 2009, Daimler was owed €5,675 million by customers, of which it expects only €5,277 million to be settled soon, either because customers have financial difficulties or they are disputing the invoice.

Inventory, also called "stock", consists of items that a company buys in order to sell them on, or make them into their products. Accounting standards require it to be recorded at the "lower of cost and net realizable value", which just means that if the items can only be sold at a loss, they need to be shown at that lower value. In most cases where items are resold, inventory is just the sum of all the cost invoices for unsold inventory. If the items are used to manufacture something else, inventory includes the cost of labour, so the figures are adjusted for work as it is done. This can be shown as "work in progress" or similar. Again from Daimler's 2009 accounts, it shows €1,517 million of raw materials, €1,626 of work in process (also known as work in progress or WIP), €9,666 million of finished goods and €36 million advance payments to suppliers.

This says that of the approximately €12.8 billion of inventory, €9.6 billion is for vehicles and spare parts ready for sale to customers, €1.5 billion for components and €1.6 billion for items in the process of being made into vehicles, including the cost of labour.

If the purchase price of identical items of inventory changes, you may need to decide which item gets sold and which remains in inventory. Suppose for example you own a petrol station, and you have taken two deliveries, 10,000 litres at €1 per litre and later another 10,000 litres at €1.10 per litre. You then sell a litre to a motorist who comes to fill up. What did that litre of petrol cost? The two main options are either to measure inventory using "FIFO" (meaning first in, first out) or average cost. So in our example, the litre you sold would be worth either €1 (being the cost of the oldest litre in inventory), or €1.05 (being the average cost of the inventory). Having decided which method to use, companies stick to that method.

Fixed assets do not have to be physically fixed to something, such as a piece of machinery screwed to a workbench. The expression comes from the idea that fixed assets are not connected with a particular transaction with a particular customer, but used many times by, and necessary for the business. For example an item of inventory only gets sold once, whereas the computer system used to generate and print the invoice is used for many transactions. So fixed assets consist of the computers, furniture, buildings and other bits of infrastructure a company owns. The value of many of these will fall in time – for example a car or a computer system will be worth less in the future than it is worth today, although a building may be worth the same or even more. To reflect this falling value, the affected assets are progressively reduced in value in the balance sheet, or depreciated, over their useful life. For example, a computer system that cost €10,000 new, and with an expected life of three years at the end of which it is worthless, would be recorded as being worth €6,666 after one year, and €3,333 after two. Whether an asset is depreciated at all, how fast (it isn't always a straight line as in this example), and over what period is something that varies from country to country and from asset to asset. So, some assets can periodically increase in value, such as a property company's land bank, or fall in value (as some mobile operators discovered when they overpaid for 3G licenses), so every year the company will decide, independent of the depreciation process, whether to adjust the value of its assets. If they are increased, it is called revaluing assets; if reduced it is called impairment. The important thing to remember is that the value of assets does not normally remain the same from one balance sheet to the next.

There are two other important items included in fixed assets: intangible assets and investments. Intangible assets are things you can't touch or see, but that have value. For example, mobile phone operators buy licenses to radio spectrum so they can offer their service, and they would hold the cost of those licenses as an intangible fixed asset. Patents and trademarks are other examples. But, rather controversially, you can use this for your own intellectual property too. The internal costs of developing software products can be listed as intangible assets, or "capitalized" (meaning make into an asset). On the face of it, that's attractive: it makes the company look stronger by increasing its assets and, as the balance sheet must always balance, increasing its shareholder funds too. In fact beefing up the balance sheet in this way (or window-dressing as it is sometimes called) can just look bad, as if the company is trying to pretend things are better than they really are.

With a majority of the world's software companies headquartered in the USA, an American accounting standard was introduced, called FAS 86, which tried to make reporting consistent by requiring software to be capitalized up to the point of technical feasibility. But this is what Oracle for example thinks of the standard, taken from their 2009 annual report: "All research and development costs are expensed as incurred. Cost eligible for capitalization under FASB Statement No.86, Accounting for the Costs of Computer Software to Be Sold, Leased, or Otherwise Marketed, were not material to our consolidated financial statements in fiscal 2009, 2008 and 2007, respectively."

In short, be careful before you capitalize. It's a bit like a drug that gives a short-term buzz, but it's difficult to kick the habit once you start.

Investments

The other important area of fixed assets is investments in other companies. This does not include short-term investments of surplus cash, but investments in or outright purchases of other companies. Companies are mostly sold for more than their book value (the value of their equity), because otherwise the actual business in terms of customers, products and brand has no intrinsic value. The difference between the price paid and the book value is called "goodwill". Companies regularly revalue their investments, especially each time the accounts are audited, to decide whether to reduce the value of the goodwill, if the value of the company purchased has been "impaired", meaning that it is now worth less than it was bought for.

It's worth looking in the notes section of company accounts at the intangible assets, because sometimes it can look a little odd, but it is relatively easy to navigate around – just remember the few simple principles. Let's look at Autonomy, a British software company, whose 2009 annual report lists five different categories of intangible assets: patents, licenses and trademarks; internally generated assets; purchased technology; customer relationships and brand names. For each category, the cost is listed plus any additions less amortization for the year. In 2009, there was a significant increase, mainly due to the acquisition of Interwoven, another technology company.

Patents and licenses are used for the day-to-day operation of the company. They can be thought of in a similar way to furniture, computer equipment or other fixed assets. Internally generated software is the capitalization of software that we looked at earlier, and this is something Autonomy decided to start doing during 2006. Purchased intangibles relate to investment acquisitions. Customer relationships and brand names also relate to acquisitions (internally created brands cannot generally be capitalized). As successful companies are normally bought for more than their equity or book value, the difference is divided into the various intangible asset categories.

Let's now look at liabilities.

Overdraft or bank borrowings are short-term banking facilities. Bank loans can appear in one of two places on a balance sheet: at the top of the current liabilities, and again in long-term liabilities or capital. There is a distinction made between these two because the first is about funding the day-to-day operations of the company while the other is considered to be part of the structural capital of the company. As the repayments mature, or are payable within the next 12 months, they are moved from long-term to short-term liabilities. As with all items on the balance sheet, all items in foreign currencies are translated at the rate of the day of the balance sheet into local currency.

Payables, also called "accounts payable" or in the UK "creditors" (the opposite of debtors), is the sum of all the invoices from suppliers that the company has received but has not yet paid, including the balances of those that have not been paid in full. Again, invoices in foreign exchange are converted at the rate of the day of the balance sheet. If you expect to receive an invoice, or perhaps items have been received but the invoice is on its way, these are not included. Instead they are listed in accruals, to be found elsewhere in the current liabilities section of the balance sheet. Invoices that are disputed are included at the value that the company thinks is the correct value, although this will need to be bottomed out at the time of the audit, at the latest. Invoices that are not due for payment in the next 12 months are shown separately as "due in more than 12 months", or similar.

Accruals reflect costs the company has incurred for which a bill has not been received. It is where adjustments are made when payments or receipts are out of sync with the normal flow of business. Suppose electricity is paid quarterly in arrears. To reflect the cost of the electricity in the accounts, the end of the first month, you accrue for the cost of a month of electricity use that has not yet been invoiced by placing that amount in "accruals". Alternatively, the electricity might instead be on a budget plan, payable quarterly in advance. In that case, the electricity that has been paid for future months is included on the asset side of the balance sheet under "pre-payments". "Accruals" are the opposite of "pre-payments" in the same way that "overdraft" is the opposite of "cash".

Accruals also include **provisions**, which are estimates of future costs such as product warranty claims by customers, or for projects that cost more to complete than estimated. With products increasingly working "out of the box", you can best find these provisions in the balance sheets of companies that build large systems. For example Ericsson, the Swedish telecoms equipment manufacturer, has provisions for warranty commitments, restructuring, project related and "other". According to Ericsson, warranty commitments "are based on historic quality rates for established products as well as estimates regarding quality rates for new products and costs to remedy the various types of faults predicted", in other words how much Ericsson expects to spend on warranty claims that have not yet been made by customers. Restructuring refers to the expected costs of redundancies and other cost reductions. Project related concern "estimated losses on onerous contracts, including probable contractual penalties". Other includes "provisions for tax issues, litigations, supplier claims and other".

Much of this is not likely to be that relevant to an entrepreneur, although making a provision for warranty claims is not a bad idea, especially if these can be made in good times. The money is not lost – if the provision is not needed, it is "released" (removed) in later balance sheets.

Deferred revenue is the next item on the balance sheet, and one that causes considerable confusion, even with experienced business people, despite the fact that the principle is easy to grasp. In essence it is work that has been invoiced but not yet carried out. If you employ a builder to work on your house, and pay him €5,000 before he starts work as a down-payment, his balance sheet before he starts work would show €5,000 as a cash asset and €5,000 as a liability in deferred revenue. It is important for technology companies such as software companies, where invoicing might be in advance or in arrears of providing the particular product or service. Revenue is "recognized" according to a set of rules.

The word "recognize" here doesn't mean to identify, but to convert a sale into a financial transaction that is acknowledged, or recognized, by accounting principles. When you receive a purchase order from a customer, nothing is affected in your accounts until you supply the customer with the product. So most companies recognize revenue at the time the product is shipped to the customer. But software in particular is harder: perhaps the customer can try it out for 30 days free of charge before deciding whether to buy; perhaps modifications need to be made to the software to meet a customer's specific needs, or perhaps the price includes periodic updates and bug fixes, or the right of the customer to ask for help under a maintenance agreement. Or perhaps the customer is going to build in the software into their product, and you, the software supplier, will receive €1 as a royalty for each of the products he sells. Although it is quite possible to devise a sensible way of deciding what is and what is not revenue, it's important to be consistent. Consistency enables companies to be more easily compared with each other, and companies can be bought or sold without having to change historical accounts to match into the acquiring company's way of doing things.

The American authorities took on the task of defining when software revenue can be recognized and over time, the principles they devised were adopted by other countries, and by international accounting standards. The following main points have been widely used:

- If the software is a standard product and does not require modification, revenue is recognized once the customer has taken delivery and cannot contractually return the product. The software supplier has raised the invoice and there is every reason to believe it will be paid in full.

- If the software needs to be written, or requires modification, revenue is recognized once the final version has been accepted by the customer, whether or not part-payments have been made. This wait for the revenue can be quite hard for companies with large projects, so it is often possible to separate the software development from its design, which is then recognized when supplied to the customer, and also to recognize any hardware at the time it is supplied.
- Support and maintenance, for example a two-year extended warranty, is recognized over the period, in this case 1/24 each month. That would mean that if the balance sheet date falls half way into the contract, for example, 12/24 of the support and maintenance fees would appear in the balance sheet as deferred revenue.

The main trap is when items are bundled. "We'll build your new ERP system for €1 million, including updates for two years" may make sense to an entrepreneur, but for an accountant or auditor, it is not good enough. The price needs to be broken down into the constituent parts (hardware, standard software, customized software, professional services, maintenance, etc.), as they are recognized differently. If there are any discounts, they need to be applied evenly across all items to prevent cross-subsidy, which might distort the revenue picture at any particular point in time. If that breakdown cannot be done, and verified by the company's independent auditor, there is a risk that the whole amount of the project cannot be recognized until the very end of the project. Something that started out as a simple attractive discount to a customer, when combined with a laudable and sensible attempt at consistency, produces an accounting trap that can create very real problems.

What about the company that receives a royalty for their software built into someone else's product? When is their revenue recognized? It is recognized when your customer ships products, and that means you may need to ask your customer for shipment information more regularly than in the business deal (they might have agreed to quarterly reporting, for example, but you might produce monthly accounts). As an alternative to royalty reporting, you can ask customers to prepay licenses in pre-defined quantities, or packs, and the more the customer buys, the cheaper they become. It's a great model for improving cash flow and getting the customer tied in.

So "deferred revenue" is an item that has been sold and invoiced, but the revenue has not yet been recognized. Whether the customer has paid makes no difference (that would just move the asset from "receivable" to "cash"). It is a liability to the company (although logically perhaps it would seem to be an asset) because it represents future profit, and profit is also on the right-hand side of the balance sheet. Remember the balance sheet sides of "assets" and "liabilities" are not "good" and "bad". A better way of looking at it is "items that need financing" and "sources of finance". Deferred revenue is a good thing; although what it eventually becomes – profit – is even better.

The final item is **equity**. This consists of share capital (the sums shareholders paid into the company to buy shares) and accumulated profits, or retained earnings. Share capital is sometimes split for legal reasons into share capital and share premium, but the latter is just the amount paid over the par value of the shares. Shares when they are created might have a value attached to them, for example €1. This is the minimum value the company can sell each share for when it is created, but has nothing to do with their value at any time afterwards.

A more important distinction within equity is between share capital and retained earnings. Share capital (including any share premium) is the amount the investors have invested in the company. Retained earnings are the accumulated after-tax profits of the company that have not been distributed to shareholders as dividends.

In some countries only retained earnings can be paid out as dividends, preventing a company from making payments to shareholders until there are cumulative profits, or "distributable reserves" because they can be distributed in the form of dividends.

What to look for in a balance sheet

- Quick sanity check: Look at the main figures in the balance sheet to understand broadly what the key items are. Look at the previous balance sheet and understand what the main changes have been.
- Simplify the balance sheet into the four main items: NFO, fixed assets, equity, and either surplus cash or loan.
  - o Financing growth: Is the NFO positive or negative? This will tell you whether the company needs funding to grow.
  - o Well financed? Calculate the Working Capital by subtracting the assets from the equity. Is this figure growing or shrinking compared with the previous period? If it is shrinking, how long will the equity last until it is extinguished?
  - o Cash usage: Compare the cash figure with the balance sheet from the previous period. How much cash did the company consume or generate in the last period? If the company has debt, how long would it take to repay the debt? If there is surplus cash, how long will it last at the current cash burn rate?
- Good or bad payers? Divide the trade account payables by the COGS figure from the P&L. This will give you the fraction of a year that the

company takes to pay a supplier's bill. Multiply that by 360 (or 180 if the P&L covers 6 months) to get the average days it takes the company to pay suppliers.
- Profitable? Did the company's equity increase or decrease in the period? Was this from trading (EBITDA), a change in fixed assets, a capital increase or some other reason? Does the company have cumulative profits?

It is important to remember that many aspects of the overall quality of a company are not reflected in the accounts, such as business risk, contractual obligations competition and competitive advantage.

The P&L helps us understand whether a business makes economic sense; is the business model improving and the company operationally sound? The balance sheet helps us understand whether a company is financially sound; what assets does the company need and have in order to operate, and is additional finance likely to be needed in the future?

Balance Sheet and P&L interaction

The P&L changes when something happens that affects the company's profits. Profits are revenue minus expenses, so the P&L only changes when sales are made or costs are incurred.

When a sale happens or an expense is incurred, the Balance Sheet also changes. When a product is sold, for example, inventory will decrease and accounts receivable increase. If the product has been sold at a profit, retained earnings will also increase.

Balance sheets always change whatever the financial transaction. In addition to changing whenever the P&L does, the Balance Sheet changes with:

- NFO changes (inventory, receivables, payables)
- Investments (buying, disposing or revaluing fixed assets, tangible and intangible)
- Capital events (raising equity, dividends, etc.).

Every time there is a financial transaction in a company, whether it is a sale or a balance sheet transaction, there is an equal and opposite one (otherwise the balance sheet would not balance any more). This concept is called double entry accounting.

It need not be between one item on each side of the balance sheet, as the example above shows (inventory and accounts receivable are both assets). Sometimes, more than one item is affected, but the principle that there are equal and opposite transactions holds, whatever the transaction. Here are some examples:

The company raises €100,000 in equity:

Assets		Liabilities & Equity	
Cash	€100,000	Equity	€100,000

It buys an asset on credit for €10,000:

Assets		Liabilities & Equity	
Fixed assets	€10,000	Payables	€10,000

The asset is depreciated by 25 per cent:

Assets		Liabilities & Equity	
Fixed assets	−€2,500	Profit	−€2,500

A product is sold for €100 that costs €25 to make:

Assets		Liabilities & Equity	
Receivables	€100		
Inventory	−€25	Profit	−€75

And so on. One side of the double entry is called "Debit" and the other side "Credit". When a customer pays, for example, you debit cash and credit receivables. Double entry accounting has its origins in the work of a 15th century Italian Friar, Luca Pacioli. He devised, or at least reported, the idea that the books or journals need to balance all the time. The reason is that for each debit there must always be an equal and opposite credit.

On and Off Balance Sheet transactions

Financial engineering can be a positive thing, despite its negative reputation. It can help shareholders to be wealthier by for example reducing the shareholder funds tied up in a company. A company that owns its office building may decide to sell the building to a financial institution and lease it back, returning the capital to shareholders.

In that example the fixed assets in the balance sheet would be reduced, with the offsetting item being an increase in cash. The company may prefer to lease or hire equipment, rather than buy it. Overseas sales offices may be owned by someone else, keeping the assets and liabilities off the main company's balance sheet, but with the sales company remaining contractually tied to the parent.

Financial engineering is open to abuse and there are extensive rules to prevent such abuses, which distort financial statements. Two friendly companies might decide to sell each other a product for €1 million. No cash needs to change hands but each company's P&L would show an increase in sales of €1 million. If they each capitalize the purchase (meaning that it appears on the balance sheet as an asset rather than be expensed through the P&L), profits would be higher in each company too. (Such revenue swaps are generally illegal.)

For example intra-group, inter-company trading, meaning two companies within the same group selling to each other, are generally excluded on consolidation to prevent revenues being exaggerated. This can reduce tax liabilities, especially if the two companies are in different countries. Company A, which is resident in a low-tax country, sells a product to Company B of the same group, which is based in a high-tax country. If Company A increases the price of the product, it will increase its profits and lower Company B's profits. The group's tax bill falls as a result. This is called transfer pricing and is a great source of business for accountants the world over.

There are many more examples of financial engineering. Much financial engineering is positive and good, limited only by the human imagination and local regulations, but it needs careful navigation.

Entrepreneurs are increasingly global, and an understanding of what is possible and allowed within an international group structure can make a great difference to the complexity, cost and tax bill of a start-up. It is unfortunately beyond the limits of this book to cover group international accounting and tax issues. After all, this is a book on finance.